Praise for *Opacities*

"Sofia Samatar's *Opacities* is simply one of the most beautiful books about writing, about being a writer, that I've ever read."   —ROSS GAY, author of *Inciting Joy*

"Sofia Samatar's *Opacities* lowers us into the deepest part of the sentence, past ruin, past the drowned, past the moon, past the future, past the writer and her ink, where the ragged dark begins to sing. *Opacities* is a posthumous book written by the living. I read this entire book in the pitch-black to keep all its brilliant secrets safe."

—SABRINA ORAH MARK, *author of Happily*

"*Opacities* fantasizes many models of writing, including the 'companion text,' the project that 'lasts your whole life,' the one that includes failure and 'deep aimlessness,' and the book that writes itself, by virtue of an accumulation of index cards in a shoebox. *Opacities* dreams of connectivity and communion. It strives to bring into correspondence the talismanic writers of the literary imaginary, and, in a voice reminiscent of the address in Chris Marker's *Sans Soleil*, Samatar conjures an anonymous, epistolary intimate. It is a book about process and ambivalence, one that ultimately evinces a deep-seated passion for the creative acts that are reading and writing."   —MOY

"*Opacities* is necessity for every person writing, reading, moving through complex spaces, lying down in fields, on beaches. Samatar turns the always-burning questions of how do we begin to write and how do we go on writing into a riveting yet diffused examination of what we have read and how we've sustained ourselves by reading. This is a book for pleasure, for travel in thought, but, perhaps, also the right thing to grab in case of emergency. It's definitely my new desert-island book."

—RENEE GLADMAN, author of *Calamities*

"*Opacities* is a writer's notebook that we get to read pre-posthumously, a conversation with the self and the dead, a gesture toward the fantasy of publication without publicity. A book for Rilke's 'narrow ledge,' full of intimacy and intensity, comforts and agitations, the haunting desires of artists."   —ELISA GABBERT, author of *Normal Distance* and *Any Person Is the Only Self*

"What is a writing method that is 'less like writing and more like living'? Sofia Samatar develops this question as a form of metallurgy in *Opacities*, a book that sets autobiography in motion until what remains is what we love the most: a notebook. Blurry, snorting, and stamping its hoof in the rain, the notebook's hybridity is both void and animal: 'Zero. Zero.' To write this bifurcated or doubled zero, Samatar thinks 'through the hole.' This is an 'incompleteness' taken to 'extremes,' and I'm here for it. Anything I could possibly write in support of this beautiful book falls short of the elation I felt when reading, something that happened in one sitting because I could not set it down." —BHANU KAPIL, author of *How to Wash a Heart*

"Was ever a darkness so refulgent as Sofia Samatar's *Opacities?* With her distinctively supple line, Samatar summons a troupe of literary night-guides from Kafka to Djebar, and leads us to the so-called vanishing point, where scarcity inverts to fullness and nothing vanishes except our certainties. Obsidian, inky, rippling, Vantablack, Samatar's vision of literature restores the dream of the night library, where we can and should read in the dark, and where the Future rises up with the face of the New Moon—her next and original face."

—JOYELLE MCSWEENEY, author of *The Necropastoral*

"In the profound company of others and in conversations with ghosts, *Opacities* is a work of great intimacy and intelligence. It is both mesmerizing and consoling to dwell in the meditative space Sofia Samatar has created. Her submerged narratives haunt (now coming to the surface, now subsiding), allowing room for the reader to enter the text in any number of ways. A most irresistible experience." —CAROLE MASO, author of *AVA* and *Mother & Child*

"*Opacities* gorgeously stages the struggle between the writer's consciousness—solitary, desiring only of the quest of its craft—and the writer as embodied, indebted to a public and to the machinations of the world of publishing. Samatar summons the testimony of a chorus of writers and thinkers in her argument against the oppression of imposed subjectivity, particularly for marginalized writers, who 'will not be granted a moment of abstraction.' Both dazzlingly intellectual and deeply felt, *Opacities* is a collection to savor and return to again and again." —LAUREN K. ALLEYNE, author of *Honeyfish*

"Sofia Samatar's *Opacities* observes the world with rare curiosity. Engaging a breadth of thinkers, Samatar considers the spiritual dimension of art-making, and offers meaningful reflections on returning to our most genuine selves. Moving seamlessly between essay and philosophy, investigation and meditation, *Opacities* is a gift."

—JAQUIRA DÍAZ, author of *Ordinary Girls*

Opacities

ALSO BY SOFIA SAMATAR

The Practice, the Horizon, and the Chain
Tone (with Kate Zambreno)
The White Mosque: A Memoir
Monster Portraits (with Del Samatar)
Tender: Stories
The Winged Histories
A Stranger in Olondria

OPACITIES

*On Writing
and the Writing Life*

SOFIA SAMATAR

SOFT SKULL  NEW YORK

First Soft Skull edition: 2024

Library of Congress Cataloging-in-Publication Data
Names: Samatar, Sofia, author.
Title: Opacities : on writing and the writing life / Sofia Samatar.
Description: First Soft Skull edition. | New York : Soft Skull, 2024. | Includes bibliographical references.
Identifiers: LCCN 2024010037 | ISBN 9781593767662 (trade paperback) | ISBN 9781593767679 (ebook)
Subjects: LCSH: Authorship. | LCGFT: Creative nonfiction.
Classification: LCC PS3619.A4496 O63 2024 | DDC 814/.6--dc23/eng/20240301
LC record available at https://lccn.loc.gov/2024010037

Cover design by Farjana Yasmin
Cover art © Kumiko Kanai / The Letter from Akiko
Book design by Wah-Ming Chang

Published by Soft Skull Press
New York, NY
www.softskull.com

Printed in the United States of America

1 3 5 7 9 10 8 6 4 2

For Kate Zambreno

Zero. Zero.

Nous réclamons pour tous le droit à l'opacité.

Édouard Glissant

I

Tonic

THE DREAM IS to create a book that will also be a tonic: not a course of study but a course of treatment. "I'm beginning a new book to have a companion," wrote Hervé Guibert, "someone with whom I can talk, eat, sleep, at whose side I can dream and have nightmares, the only friend whose company I can bear at present." He had been reading *The Pillow Book of Sei Shōnagon* in the country. Shivering with cold, he bit into an overly salty biscuit. I copied his words and sent them to you by email, including his parentheses: "(Living with a book, even when one isn't writing it, is altogether marvelous.)" That's what we were looking for, the *altogether marvelous*. I wrote to you of a writing method: Take notes on index cards and put them in a shoebox. When the box is full, the book is done. This method seemed to me comforting. We were searching for a writing method that was less like writing and more like living. I really want to write my next book that way, I wrote to you, as notes that can take in everything: a Compleat or commonplace book, a companion text. It would be a handbook, I wrote. The book you keep ready to hand. A circadian practice, a gentle dependency. You'd live with this dream text as with some necessary daily drug. You'd sit up with it—or it would sit up with you—as one sits up with the dying.

"THIS IS WHAT is diabolical about prose, it is never finished," said Flaubert, cooling his cheeks with the palms of his hands, then cooling his hands against the iron knobs of the tall andirons. But we weren't afraid of the diabolical; on the contrary, we desired it. I, for instance, was inspired by Aimé Césaire, who published at least three versions of his *Notebook of a Return to the Native Land* between 1939 and 1947. Perpetual magic: a never-ending book. A sustained delirium of rotting straw, obsessive bells, and rain. You, too, you wrote, were entranced by impossible projects, by books that are never written and books that never end. You wrote to me of the nineteenth-century tradition of the deathbed memoir, a book dictated from one's final pillow. It was utopian, diabolical, ideal. Once, I wrote to you, the internet seemed to promise me an interminable scroll. And there were the social connections, too, branching across space. But then I became disgusted with my name. Now I feel more intensely than ever the desire for an endless text. It's the only solution to the problem of literature. Only when a book ends and is published does it enter the realm of the name. If you never finished a text, you'd never wind up there, in what I called, perhaps with a hint of hysteria, the *blood-soaked arena* of the publishing world. The best book, I wrote, would be the one that lasts your whole life. At some point, you would simply leave it behind.

I THINK WE had been almost stunned by publishing. It sent us into retreat. But we tried to be generous with our younger selves, the ones who thought it impossible that they would ever be published, for whom publication was the one thing, the consuming desire. Back then, I confessed, when no one was paying attention to my writing, I habitually drew attention to my person. In retrospect this seemed to me low, shameful. I am trying to say, I wrote to you, that I am not above any of this. I still felt embroiled in it: the name, the skin, the color, the gender expression, the cultural practice I called *the diversity sideshow*, the question of whether confession was a source of radical power or a trap that sewed one up in one's own carcass, the question of whether it was in fact shameful to draw attention to one's race and gender in literary discussions or whether what was really shameful was leaving these things out, and the possibility that the idea of literature as a privileged spiritual ground was romantic, reactionary, dangerous, and dumb.

YOUR FRIEND WANTED to plan a book party for you; you said you wanted a book burial instead. Bury the book. Throw it away. Publicity agonizes. You wrote to me of Goethe abandoning the court and running away to Italy, shifting his existence and his writing out of people's sight, traveling under a false name to escape the author of *Werther*. There he would learn to draw, he would learn at last to write again, to hear the half-obliterated groaning of the spirits. Rilke hid behind his poems, then tried to hide his poems behind his hair, his hands, or any opaque object. He dimmed the passages with his breath. He made himself small, he hid as children hide, he raised a brief and happy cry. "Only an angel," he wrote to himself and to us, "should have been allowed to look for you. But if then you cautiously glanced up, there was no doubt that they had seen you all the time, everybody in that hateful, hollow, peering hall: you, you, you, and nothing but you."

I REALIZED THAT there was a tyranny of identity experienced by all authors, and a second tyranny reserved for those with representational bodies. The exemplars. *Exemplary*: serving as a desirable model; characteristic of its kind; serving as a warning or deterrent.

TO BE ASKED to speak or write as a representation of a category causes woe. It was like being in mourning for something. I wondered what I was mourning, what I lacked moving through the fluorescent conference light with my name tag, my paper cup. I realized it was writing.

I FELT MYSELF becoming antisocial, but what does *so-cial* mean? *Social* can mean "being-forced-to-appear." To be made visible, and only in certain ways. Flatly, as a logo or a tag. To understand this, it's necessary to scrape off the web of gratitude. You must peel the gratitude off your eyes. I said I would peel myself away. I'd go from appealing to a peeling. Until the cracks and fissures were covered with songs. And so my models became those who were not interested in appeal. Alejandra Pizarnik wrote, "My name, my pronoun—a gray void." And Édouard Glissant didn't even want to see straight: "Give up this old obsession with discovering what lies at the bottom of natures." It was a recoil from transparency. A dread not of being seen but of being caught. Devoured. I felt shriveled up, blistered by sudden light. I felt flung down in the bottom of a boat. Scrabbling. And then the restaurant. They ate their salads. I watched them through the glass.

BUT IF WE break the glass, thought the dispossessed, they'll run roughshod over us. It was a problem of proximity. Is this too much to ask: to be close enough to the other that he can hear you, but not so close that he's biting your face off?

I HAD UNFORTUNATE plans, I drove myself into a state, I was in a frenzy. I would write the INAUTHENTICITY MANIFESTO. We the undersigned are tired of being black at literary events. We reserve the right to have no identity, like Keats. We reserve the right to say "Keats." We perceive ourselves in Deleuze and Guattari's *Kafka: Toward a Minor Literature*. Even the phrase *minor literature* makes us inordinately happy. We are jumping up and down like a bunch of kids. Big pieces of ice fly up from under our feet. Just as we are nomads and immigrants in relation to language, so we are traitors and clowns in relation to this panel on diversity in literature. We will settle for nothing less than the whole field of desire and history. We exceed ourselves, we deterritorialize, we escape. We are Hilton Als when he says, "This is my farewell." We're Hilton Als when he's Joni Mitchell's autobiography. Thank you for saying you liked my book and would put it on the syllabus if you were ever granted your dream course on Global Fantasies. Why not teach it in your regular literature course? It reminds me of a dream I had, that I woke up somewhere and a tall, calm woman gave me a beauty treatment. She handed me a rough brush to curry my legs, as if I were a horse, and a comb to smooth the hair down afterward. She rubbed in satiny powder. It's clear you're African, she said, or anyway, of Global Descent.

THE PROBLEM WITH manifestoes is their language. That's sad, because they're made of language. It's sad when your problem is nothing but you. I woke up and I was running beside a horse. He turned to me and said, "Here we are on Wuthering Heights." The ice in the forest was cracked where the children had been playing. I could see the mountains, very dark, with little trails coming down. That's where we were going, toward the fog. The problem with manifestoes is that they're too literal. They lend themselves to schisms, clubs, intolerant friend gangs, all the things I hate. The death of language: this, as much as its birth, is accomplished in groups. I was hanging large pale emblems on my arms. How was I going to run with these things? Instead of a manifesto, I'd like to write a magic spell. When I finished writing it, I'd break into a million pieces. And you, too, when you finished reading, you'd break into a million pieces. A spell for shattering, so that everyone could live in the world of art. My visions are naïve, like the dreams of horses. In the clatter of hoofbeats, half-thawed chunks of writing were flowing down the hills.

THE LETTERS WERE what remained when we had largely withdrawn from the public sphere. We wrote often, sometimes several times a day. Flurries. You called it a *buoyant fugue state*. My friend K'eguro called it "doing an Emily Dickinson": to disappear from the blogs, the social media, the writing for general consumption, the commentary on current events, on the scandals and debates of the publishing world, to stop being, or trying to be, in whatever small way, a public figure, to no longer keep one's name in a place where it had a good chance of being passed around, to no longer say things in spaces where the goal was to be repeated but to go on writing to friends, to write intensively to friends, pouring out everything there, the thoughts, the quotations, the cries. It was a way to stay alive as a writer. We exchanged confidences and confidence. You said it was when you were most a writer: in letters to other writers. I quoted Kafka: "Writing letters is actually an intercourse with ghosts and by no means just with the ghost of the addressee but also with one's own ghost, which secretly evolves inside the letter one is writing."

IT WAS A WAY of continuing to speak even when one felt completely flayed. Too raw to withstand a glance.

THE PROBLEM WITH giving up the family name is that you might lose your family. You might withdraw from the women's conference where all your friends are. Once, you told me that you were a writer partly because you missed people: to speak to a community of ghosts. You quoted Theresa Hak Kyung Cha's *Audience Distant Relative*. Her story was almost too hard for me to bear. She entered between the two white columns. White and stone. Abrasive. She bought a ticket. It was 6:35 p.m. "you are the audience / you are my distant audience / i address you / as i would a distant relative." She handed her ticket to the usher and climbed three steps, into the room. The whiteness of the screen took her backward almost half a step. "as if a distant relative / seen only heard only through someone else's description." How, you asked, can a book contain the furious energy of its failure, its processes, its drafts, its many notebooks? How can a book contain and name a community, with all its fragments and fractures? This strange kin group, related yet unknown.

"MY PEOPLE," Kafka said, "provided that I have one."

PERHAPS WHAT WE were searching for, you wrote
to me, was a way to write toward a "negative community: the community of those who have no community."
That was Maurice Blanchot quoting Georges Bataille.
That was Blanchot describing "the anonymity of the
book." A book that doesn't address anyone, he wrote,
a book without an audience, with no destination except
the unknown, and he began copying from the book beside him, *The Malady of Death* by Marguerite Duras.
You wouldn't know her, he wrote, you'd have seen her
everywhere at once, in a hotel, in a street, in a train, in
a bar, in a book, in a film, in yourself, in your inmost
self, this nameless recipient with her tall, long body
who sleeps in a bed, and he watches her sleep as sor-
row grows in the room, in the sound of the sea, and
when she wakes he asks her, how can loving happen,
the emotion of loving, and she tells him, only through
a mistake. Love comes through a lapse in the logic of
the universe, never an act of will. Until that night he
hadn't realized how ignorant one might be of what the

eyes see, the hands and body touch. Facing the black sea, leaning against the wall of the room where she was sleeping, he wept for himself as a stranger might.

THE BLACK SEA under a sky bleached of light. The rising water. A fine drizzle falling. The sadness of Georges Bataille. "These notes link me like Ariadne's thread to my fellow creatures and the rest seems vanity to me. However I cannot give them to any of my friends to read."

"CORRESPONDENCE," WROTE Theresa Hak Kyung Cha. "To scatter the words."

"NO POEM IS intended for the reader," wrote Walter Benjamin, "no picture for the beholder, no symphony for the listener." Reading this, I remembered his practice of lifting quotations from texts, which he cherished as if they had been written for him alone.

"(THE PRINCIPLE OF INCOMPLETENESS)," Blanchot jotted in parentheses. It made me think of Haytham El Wardany, who dreamed of a secret society of artists who lived and wrote according to this principle: the League of Incomplete Literature. Once, I had sent you his description of this curious group. "In their eyes," El Wardany explained, "completed works conceal the incompleteness at their heart by way of an artificial unity: a unity whose purpose is to rescue their author. Incomplete works, however, are quite unashamed of this incompleteness. Indeed, they take it to its extreme as if to say, 'You can never write alone.'" He entered the Sukkariyyah Café, pulled out one of the wooden chairs, and seated himself at a cheap latticework table. The windows were closed against the cold. The embroidered hangings spoke of better days. The noise was immense: members of the League babbling, interrupting each other. Every new story split, unfinished, cut off without complaint. Was there, then, a necessary link between community and incompleteness? Was the desire for a never-ending book, which I had thought so personal, even individualistic, related to this need for others? I thought again of the deathbed memoir, which must be dictated. And in the Sukkariyyah Café, the din increased, the voices of the League entangled with all the sounds of the city, mingled with roaring traffic, whipcracks, wailing children, barking dogs, alarms, a noise that swelled to an almost unbearable point before giving way to an ocean of silence in which the fragments were absorbed.

I WISHED TO take my incompleteness to extremes. I wanted never to write alone. I thought of Clarice Lispector, who was about to begin to exist. "During the time I'm writing and speaking," she explained, "I'm going to have to pretend that someone is holding my hand."

AT THIS TIME, I began to imagine what I called *the project of nothing*. A project of deep aimlessness and anonymity. Without knowing what it would look like, I felt that this project was urgent, perhaps especially for "us." For those who say "us."

I REREAD A story you'd sent me from the notebooks of Daniil Kharms. It's about a red-haired man who completely disappears. He's called a red-haired man but he doesn't have red hair or anything else. To me, this story was like a recipe or blueprint. In other words, I received it as a person seeking instruction. Daniil Kharms instructed himself, following Gogol, to write something down, even if it's just the fact that there's nothing to write, and he really did write in his notebook, "Today I wrote nothing. Doesn't matter." How can the *nothing* and *doesn't matter* spread until writing is freed and becomes like a holiday? Meanwhile, Can Xue was writing applications, which she called "creations," all over the houses of the town. She covered the walls with chalk. No one understood these writings, which were fragmented, repetitive, and excessively long. Can Xue gained experience. "Sometimes," she wrote, "to achieve oblivion, you have to be noticed. Then people will start leaving you alone." She picked up a coin from a flagstone and flung it with all her might into a distant thicket. After the collapse, she enjoyed a long period of quiet.

THE PROJECT OF nothing, I thought, would be an opening out, a discipline. As in a yoga practice—except that sounded silly. Then again, silly things can be moving. It's moving when Jim Lyons writes in his notebook, "Empathy as a theme. Empathy and more—the idea that each person carries within them the possibility the truth of a million different people. Old, young, male, female, black, white, gay, straight, sick, well, sad, happy, powerful, powerless, crazy, sane, brilliant, foolish, tyrant, victim." NEW YORK CITY through the windows. Colored lights stained the wet black streets. The Christmas season. Not to keep consolidating and shoring up one's identity. Instead to identify outward, into the kitchen, very white, with accents of black and silver stainless steel. CLOSE ON ANDY'S HANDS. As he takes a teacup off the shelf. Jim Lyons lay in the hospital reading Andy Warhol's diaries. "Since I was a boy," he wrote, "I have felt keenly that the specifics of my body were disconnected from the person I felt I was." Detached, he drifted into the dark TV room, heart of the unmade film. The blue light flickered across his face as he changed the channels. Like traveling into the labyrinth of the brothel-museum where Roberto Calasso saw that the history of literature is a sinuous garland of plagiarism. Allusion, citation, parody, translation, tribute, I wrote to you, and you wrote back to me, it's all I think about. This happened several times, that we passed certain phrases back and forth, the talismanic ones, exchanging them like mantras. As if to achieve an amplification of the longed-for thought. Or to absorb it until it was *here*, forgotten. The beautiful blond man on the TV, androgynous and stoned. Amber, sapphire, magenta lights across his skin. "Not what's inside," he was saying. "Never. That you can't film." A piercing whistle shattered the stillness, waking Jim Lyons from his dream. He went to take the kettle off the burner. CLOSE on the clear steaming water pouring into the white teacup. If it's not possible to film the inside, then what are you filming? How close can you get? Are you doomed to objectify the other? The risk of throwing off the proper name—yes, it can fail, I wrote, but for me it re-creates the feeling of my most intense moments of reading. That dissolution, the blurring of the edges of the self. It's all I want from writing: an incandescent reading. A gray line of moisture made his T-shirt cling to his torso. As if his wound was weeping. "Too big?" he wondered. "How to start?"

AND PERHAPS IT was this desire for the large, for boundless fluidity, that drew us toward the desiccated hermits. A passion that was difficult to explain. I thought of Deleuze and Guattari, their claim that the lonely bachelor in Kafka's diaries doesn't flee the world. Instead, he makes it take flight. I copied lines into my notebook: "The highest desire desires both to be alone and to be connected to all the machines of desire." I was startled by the tapping of their words, a peculiar rattling sound, very lively but very regular. "A machine that is all the more social and collective insofar as it is solitary, a bachelor, and that, tracing the line of escape, is equivalent in itself to a community whose conditions haven't yet been established." Perhaps, I thought, you and I were simply a pair of bachelor machines. Deleuze and Guattari jumped up and down in my room like twin celluloid balls. White balls with blue stripes. When one of them touched the floor the other was in the air, a game they continued to play without stopping.

TO BELONG TO a community whose conditions haven't yet been established—it is to be so alone. And, in fact, it's worse than that. You don't *belong* to this community, you're *equivalent to it*. How I would like to have a little dog! But every time I think of getting a dog, I think of the dirt, the fleas, and then the inevitable illnesses it would suffer, how it sits in a corner or limps about, whimpers, coughs, chokes from some pain, I wrap it in a rug, whistle a little melody, offer it milk, in short I nurse it in the hope that this, as indeed is possible, is nothing but a passing sickness, while it may be a serious, disgusting, and contagious disease. I can't bear to have a sick old dog.

YOU CAN'T HAVE a dog without having a sick old dog. At night, your wound weeps. Your T-shirt clings. You are dissolving. Mortal.

"LET US NOT desert one another," Jane Austen urged that anonymous group, her fellow novelists. "We are an injured body."

II

Box

THESE ARE JUST notes for another book, the one I wanted to write. Overwhelmed by the difficulties of form, I had, at the time, begun to make notes on index cards, which I kept in a large cardboard box. I sent you a photograph of the box. The method, I warned, had turned out to be terrible. I called it the Nightmare Tarot. To write on index cards was one thing, to organize them another. I didn't want to write notes *for* stories but notes *as* stories. You, too, you wrote, longed for works that were notebooks, sketchbooks. You reminded me of Bhanu Kapil's *Schizophrene*, the way she takes her notebook and throws it into the dark garden, into the snowy garden, into the wet grid. That's what I wanted: to throw my notecards out. To throw them away and then, somehow, retrieve them. Somehow to retain their atmosphere, their ragged smell, that sense of something gathered, hoarded, of the *stash*. As you wrote: *a work suffused with feeling.* Doorway, early afternoon. A wet snow falling on the ruins. You took notes with such energy, such passion, but that can't be writing, can it? I replied that no one respects a notebook until the writer is dead. It was here that I fell on the notion of posthumous writing. When I say I want to write my next book like a posthumous text, I wrote to you, I mean: as a notebook, with that kind of feel. The feel of something found after the writer has departed, notes for an unwritten manuscript, or, even better, some juvenilia, a marbled composition book from the days when writing was the great joy and shame, when it had to be hidden at all costs, on pain of death, and I could see that this was childish, and perhaps what we had been calling a return to the self, this rejection of the public stage, was a kind of regression, oriented toward childhood, when there was no expectation that one would take the floor, and it was so easy to disappear, under bushes, in bed. Something juvenile about notebooks, scrapbooks, smaller and smaller fragments, tiny writing. She flung her book outside and it got ruined. Reading under the covers with a flashlight, is that a poetics? I would like to be infantile, I wrote.

RESEARCH, BELOVED ENEMY, abhorred love. I couldn't stop taking notes. I think the fiction is research, you wrote to me, I think the research is fiction. It was true, the research felt like fiction, unfettered like a novel, it kept opening everywhere, it was a world. And like a novel it always threatened to be a waste of time. What is it *for?* I asked myself, copying lines. "The collector lives a piece of dream-life," wrote Walter Benjamin. I was afraid of becoming one of those people. One of those who never finishes anything, the rejected ones, the failed doctoral students, the little dried-up people in libraries, fussy, addicted to weird rituals developed long ago, perhaps to survive something, and now calcified, inescapable. One of those pitiful beings that doesn't PRODUCE. This fear coexisted with my desire for a never-ending book. The fear seemed perfectly at home with the desire. Or perhaps it's better to say the desire was coiled up in the fear. I had my methods: the dog-eared pages and the little check marks in pencil, then the sentences copied onto index cards or notebooks, then the notebook pages copied and cut and pasted into new notebooks. It wasn't just the amount of material that induced vertigo, it was the pleasure of a process that threatened to become an end in itself. The physical, mechanical pleasure of marking the page where something had been seen. As if one were not a writer but a data-mining robot. "The writing consists largely of quotations," Benjamin wrote of his work, "the craziest mosaic technique imaginable." It was the most banal, most fleeting, most sentimental, weakest hour of his life. An everyday hour, the night, the lost twittering of birds. He drew a breath at the sill of the open window. He would not sleep. He was on a blind, senseless, frenzied quest for happiness. It shone from his eyes; they were not happy, but in them lay fortune as it lies in gambling or love. "Nothing was more characteristic of him in the thirties," Hannah Arendt wrote, "than the little notebooks with black covers which he always carried with him and in which he tirelessly entered in the form of quotations what daily living and reading netted him in the way of 'pearls' and 'coral.'"

YOU WROTE TO me of a book that would be a catalogue of obsessions. It reminded me of what Coleridge wrote about Sir Thomas Browne: that Browne was a Hunter of Oddities and Strangenesses, whose oeuvre was a collection, a Museum and Cabinet of Rarities. Such a mesmerizing fantasy: a book that makes itself. You simply add to it, a little bit every day. A dream of the artist as magpie or wandering child or comfortable man with many hours: a dream of creation without suffering. I was reading an interview with the filmmaker Theo Angelopoulos and watching fuzzy YouTube clips of his *Voyage to Cythera*. A ship in foam. An old man dancing, turning, lifting his arms, his only music the thin clap of another's hands. Blue translucent segments, frame by frame. A series in motion. It was both a journey and an image museum. I wrote to you that Angelopoulos said a film, despite its failures and omissions, remains a record of an intellectual journey: an inventory.

A SERIES OF blocks, I wrote to you, solid and illuminated like windows. This was the text of my desire.

I SENT YOU a photograph of *The Letter from Akiko* by the artist Kumiko Kanai, which was then on exhibit in a Tokyo gallery: a box with compartments housing brightly colored miniatures, toys, and small framed drawings. In this box, which is also a letter, glazed and shabby surfaces nestle together: a doll-size plastic cauliflower, a red felt horse. I sent it to you because it's possible that the artist is the sister of the writer Mieko Kanai, who wrote about an impossible photograph, a photograph-as-collection that could contain "all the fascination that the eternity of the instant holds." She was drinking her second coffee in the dining car of an express train heading north. The sun was setting behind the forest. She tore up a cigarette pack and wrote inside it: "My first camera was a toy tin one of the old lens-shutter type that my father had given me for my seventh birthday." *The Letter from Akiko* gleams with objects that seem both stray and precious. Tiny clothespins. A watering can. A drawing of a guillotine. "The aperture was limited to either eight or eleven, and the view through the four millimeter-diameter finder looked like a scene from inside a small window with a rectangular black frame." A private snapshot sent from one friend to another. Whether or not the two artists were sisters, I thought *The Letter from Akiko* would appeal to the writer Kanai, who wanted to capture the very life of the instant. The magnetism of this box of fragments, and its frailty. Like an interior accidentally glimpsed from the window of a train. At first, she wrote, she didn't know what to photograph with the new camera. "In fact, I thought it incredible that one could take a picture with that little box."

WHAT WAS A photograph? Kanai wondered. A question that touches the heart of writing, at least for a certain type of writer, the writer-collector. "Wasn't it simply that a part of the world had been peeled away, and made a stain there? A stain of light."

ONE THING I knew was that I would never be a good content provider. I would have liked to become a form provider. I quoted M. John Harrison, who said we value the films of Andrei Tarkovsky "for the way he chooses then irradiates the objects of his concern." I wanted to irradiate my chosen objects, but how was this to be done in writing—that is, in the dark? Camera obscura: the dark chamber. You told me you were thinking through the role of art and literature, and accidentally I read *thinking through the hole*. Thinking through the hole of art as if it were a crawl space or a window. I wanted art to be a building and a hole. When it comes to writing, there's always a longing for objects, I wrote to you, that's why we speak of chopping, unfolding, nesting one thing inside another. Isn't all this an attempt to conceive of writing as an object? If it's not an object, why would we speak of *form*? I wrote to you of Benjamin's three stages of prose writing: the musical, the architectonic, and the textile. So first you have a song and at the end you have a piece of cloth and in between there's something like a shelter. It was a desire for *every mode*. Uncompromising thirst. It was Baudelaire, "Which of us, in his moments of ambition, has not dreamed of the miracle of a poetic prose, musical, without rhythm and without rhyme, supple enough and rugged enough to adapt itself to the lyrical impulses of the soul, the undulations of reverie, the shocks of consciousness?" I only wish I was stronger, I wrote, more gifted, better educated, but in the end my weakness changes nothing, I have to do what I'm doing, to go on producing my "repetitive scraps," I wrote, like the beggar in Ousmane Sembène's *Xala* dropping his shreds of music all over the street, and writing this I recalled that this monotonous, buzzing beggar was in fact the moral conscience of the city, which made me wonder if there was something wrongheaded about the search for form, and I remembered that Benjamin also instructed himself, when writing his *Arcades Project*, to "say something about the method of composition itself: how everything one is thinking at a specific moment in time must at all costs be incorporated into the project at hand," and what could this *at all costs* mean but a threat, a threat to form itself, the menace of impending damage in the service of things, random and arbitrary things that, needing to be incorporated into the project then at hand, would twist it, bulge it, deform it, unmake it?

I WANTED TO send you something very small and perfect that would say everything. A single sentence. A
word. A letter.

CLARICE LISPECTOR: "The day I manage a form as impoverished as I am inside, instead of a letter, I think I've already told you, you'll receive a small box full of Clarice dust."

I REMEMBERED THOSE who got fed up with form. Frantz Fanon, who declared: "I shall be derelict." Hélène Cixous, her cry: "And why don't you write? Write! Writing is for you, you are for you; your body is yours, take it." Take it, seize this writing that is your body. Its form is flesh. Its form is gesture, said Antonin Artaud, who wanted us to quit messing around with style and be instead "like victims burnt at the stake, signaling through the flames." Desire to stop thinking about it, throw off the shackles of intent and say what *is*. It's not anti-intellectual, it comes from a kind of exhaustion, from the wretched, stumbling fatigue of those worn out in useless quests who finally sit down in the wilderness and eat stones. To their surprise, these stones are edible. They have a taste. "Write without making corrections," said Marguerite Duras. By this time she had sailed in vain all around the Java Sea, among the Indonesian Cyclades, toward Pontianak, in the Natuna archipelago. At last she lay down on the deck of her hired boat and asked for her body to be taken to Singapore. For several days she lay there dead on the deck. "One ought to eject what one writes, manhandle it, almost," she wrote, "yes, treat it roughly, not try to trim profusion but let it be part of the whole, and not tone down anything either, whether its speed or its slowness, just leave everything as it is when it appears."

I UNDERSTOOD THAT some of the writers I quoted, like Fanon and Cixous, were frustrated not by general questions of form but by the specific problems that arose from being shut out of a literary tradition, the walls raised against women and colonized people. Yet I wondered whether what Kafka called "the impossibility of writing German" was of greater concern than "the impossibility of writing." And whether, perhaps, what ought to concern us most was what pierced Fanon and Cixous, certainly, as much as Kafka: *the impossibility of not writing.*

THIS NOTEBOOK FEELS like something moving in waves. It keeps on shifting back and forth between appearance and disappearance. The disappearance dance, I called it once. It's like a curtain flapping ceaselessly before an open window. Again, I wrote, the desire to disappear meets the desire to be seen. I was reading Bhanu Kapil's *Ban en Banlieue*. She was sitting with Petra Kuppers in the café in Berkeley that served vegan chocolate cake in 2011. "I am not interested in disclosure," Petra Kuppers told her. "I am interested in discharge." Words you and I would exchange several times in letters, moving a cursor to a place on the screen to induce the discharge of *send*. I don't want to reject confessional writing outright, I wrote to you, but it's a tricky mode for works received as black or feminist texts, autoethnography is expected of us, you get that voyeuristic thing where people are really looking for confession, trying to root it out, and it's fetishistic, brutal, I wrote, one is deprived of philosophy, I'm less interested in "what happened to you" than the transmission of a feeling, something breathable and contagious, a vast, raw, yet untethered emotion, that's how I want to be seen and how I want the writers I love to be seen, not for the self but for the ecstasy, the writerly ecstasy, caught and passed on like an electric charge.

"THERE IS MUCH I cannot tell you," Clarice Lispector wrote. "I am not going to be autobiographical. I want to be 'bio.'"

FOR SEVERAL DAYS I carried around the words of M. NourbeSe Philip: "The purpose of avant-garde writing for a writer of color is to prove you are human." These words distressed me because, although some people saw me as an object, I was not very interested in subjectivity. I was ashamed of my reluctance to prove I was human. I felt like a hypocrite when I taught my students to distrust the post-structuralist turn of the 1960s. It was simply too much of a coincidence, I told my students, that just as colonized people were demanding and achieving their independence, just as they were forcing the imperial warlords to recognize them as legal humans, writers in France began preaching the death of the subject. This was true, but it was rich coming from me, as I asked nothing better than to completely die as a subject. I felt stopped up by these contradictions, dumb. This sense of dumbness, I wrote to you, might be where culture becomes visible. You know your culture is happening to you when you find it impossible to speak. Otherwise you can trick yourself, feel like an individual with agency, blah blah, as long as you can talk, but when you're blocked, hemmed in, then you know where you are. If you asked me, what is the sound of culture, I would say: a subdued howling.

WAS IT THE way our work was read, pinioned in the tight bands of identity politics, that made us so eager and so afraid to disappear? No, I wrote to you once, it has to be more than that, because I've always had this feeling, even before I was published. I've always been drawn to this matrix: dissolution / ecstasy / unbeing / object / self-as-object / abjection / multiplicity / THING. It's the reason I began reading Rilke twenty years ago, for his dark sobs, his knowledge that "Every angel is terrifying." I wanted that obliterating touch. To be the traveler coming down from the mountains into the valley, bearing some pure word, the yellow and blue gentian. I sent you, several times, these words of Goethe's: "There is a tender empiricism that makes itself so inwardly identical with the object that it thereby becomes true theory." Anything, felt closely enough, could be the angel. But how difficult it was to say: house, pitcher, fruit tree, window.

I DON'T KNOW how to be still thinking through things, you wrote to me. The thoughts are like constantly nervous energy, electricity, I cannot catch them. My friend Ashon wrote to me that he had been reading an essay on Walter Benjamin by Susan Buck-Morss and thinking about vibration. "Think of the central nervous system and how it is discontinuous," Ashon wrote. "Our sense perception .of the world is grounded in the fact of our flesh's discontinuous nature: nerve endings are detached and information must leap, must jump, must produce choreographies of encounter with other nerve endings." Sometimes, like you, I could not catch my thoughts. Everything was going too fast. I loved these moments, although I lost so much in them. To feel a prickling of fervid static all along one's skin. The hand was pressed, too slow, it couldn't keep up with the mind. Stuck somewhere with no computer, writing to you on my phone, I tried to say that for me our letters had been a tremendous source of energy, but my fingers were too reckless and the autocorrect function flashed out *tremendous soirée, tremendous spires, tremendous seizure.* What a tremendous seizure it's been, I wrote. "Vibration," Ashon told me, "is what allows us to sense that we are, in fact, touching, though such a fact is really only ever a metaphor." Later that night I wrote in my notebook: *the persistence of enchantment*.

WHEN I READ the essay by Susan Buck-Morss, I learned that Kant claimed the statesman and the general are both superior to the artist because they shape reality, while artists just shape representations. We, the artists, are false gods. And because in the modern era God is dead, it is incumbent on human beings to step into his role. We ought to be moving mountains, not by miracles but by machines, perhaps by fracking, I thought, wondering if Kant would approve. This clarified for me the words of Leonora Carrington: "If I remember correctly writers usually find some excuse for their books, although why one should excuse oneself for having such a quiet and peaceful occupation I really don't know. Military people never seem to apologize for killing each other yet novelists feel ashamed for writing some nice inert paper book that is not certain to be read by anybody." This was precisely the problem: the uncertainty of reading. It was the dilemma of engaged literature. One simply could not be sure what a book might do, or if it would do anything at all. Writing is flimsy, suspect, most likely a waste of time. And for this—for a hobby!—we've abdicated the throne.

We've given up our role as gods. No wonder the shame is so deep, so all-encompassing, I thought. No wonder we look to commitment to justify and cleanse our passion. Writing is failure on a cosmic scale.

MANY WRITERS I KNEW claimed they would be satisfied if their books made life more bearable for just one person. But you can't be sure of that. Not even if the person is you.

THE ARTIST AND WRITER Alfred Kubin was disappointed that he never illustrated one of Kafka's novels, which touched him so deeply. He met Kafka once, in Prague, in 1912. However, according to Kubin's biographer, the two artists spoke only about their hypochondria. Reading this, I felt a rush of fellow feeling. How often, in our letters, writing about writing looked like the record of a series of physical ailments. I'm either writing slowly or I'm choking, you wrote to me, and I wrote to you: I just want to get through this, it's like I'm having some kind of illness. It seemed we never finished our books; instead, we recovered from them. You wrote that you often thought of writing as a sickness, after Wittgenstein, who wrote, in a friend's copy of the *Tractatus Logico-Philosophicus*: "Each one of these sentences is the expression of a disease." As the train started off, Alfred Kubin looked out the window and caught a final glimpse of the high wall, black against the night sky. It was a melancholy journey. First there was the fog, which made breathing difficult, and then the smoky oil lamp, enough to make a man sick. I don't know why this seemed like the best way to talk about writing, or why, as I wrote the words *weariness, suffocation, fever,* it gave me such a sense of lightness, almost of elation. Completing a draft, I wrote giddily, is like being hit in the face. I feel concussed, I wrote, the book is glaring in my eyes, I can't see a thing. Perhaps it was as Can Xue suggested, that "one's body is most vibrant when one's disease reaches its last stage." As for Kafka, he was careful to record his talk with Kubin, as if transcribing the secrets of literary production. "The artist Kubin recommends Regulin as a laxative, a powdered seaweed that swells up in the bowels, shakes them up, is thus effective mechanically in contrast to the unhealthy chemical effect of other laxatives which just tear through the excrement and leave it hanging on the walls of the bowels."

THE WAY TO talk about writing was as a sadness of the flesh. Kubin resting his foot on his knee to trim the frayed edge of his trousers. Later, seeing Kafka's limp arm lying on the table, he cried out, "But you are really sick!" The way to talk about writing was to recognize collapse. How one could never be a god, even a false one. The frankness of such language was a relief. It drew me close. "When someone is vomiting," wrote Marguerite Duras, "you hold him tenderly."

I WAS READING Bruno Schulz because my friend
Rosalind had sent me one of his letters, which I imme-
diately passed on to you. In the letter, Schulz described
how his stories came to life when ordinary objects around
him began to "wink" or "radiate." "The first seed of my
story 'Birds,'" he explained, "was a certain flickering of
the wallpaper, pulsating in a dark field of vision." Shortly
after the wallpaper began to pulse, the birds arrived, fill-
ing the rooms with splashes of crimson, verdigris, silver.
Their king was an ancient condor with a stony, dignified
profile that used the same chamber pot as Schulz's father.
I remembered James Joyce at the Ormond Hotel, seated
at the bronzegold bar, dreaming of pearls. And Clarice
Lispector, who wrote, "What beautiful music I can hear
in the depths of me. It is made of geometric lines criss-
crossing in the air. It is chamber music. Chamber music has no melody. It is a way of expressing the silence.
I'm sending you chamber writing." All the surfaces un-
dulated, scintillant. The birds perched on the curtain
rods, the wardrobes, the hanging lamps. "Have you

ever noticed," asked Schulz, "swallows rising in flocks from between the lines of certain books, whole stanzas of quivering pointed swallows? One should read the flight of these birds . . ."

SO WRITING WILL be a body and a dwelling. Box with aperture. Edged and moving. Crossing over. Condor, camera, train. I wrote to you of the nineteenth-century tightrope walker Madame Saqui, who was still performing in her sixties, when according to a newspaper she was "decripid, poor and old." "The day of the Venetian Fête was stormy, with wind, rain and heavy squalls from the sea. At four in the afternoon, the hour fixed for madame's exhibition, it blew almost a hurricane. The rope quivered in the gale. With her costume (an enchanter's robe, with flowing sleeves and a long white beard), and her flesh-less frame, she was altogether as light a body as one of Mr. Waterton's owls stuffed with cotton wool." This Mr. Waterton, I learned, was a famous taxidermist. Madame Saqui was as light as an owl already dead. Writing will be so light. "The written word will take flight from the pa-tio," wrote Assia Djebar, "will be tossed from a terrace." Assia Djebar was a little girl taking refuge under the medlar trees. She was climbing up to count the pigeons in the loft, she was breathing the smell of the carobs in the shed, of the hay trampled by the mare's hooves when she was let out into the field. Writing will be like that, it will escape. A scrap of paper. A crumpled cloth. A servant girl's hand in the dark. You feel how it involves the whole body, I wrote. Throwing, reaching. She would compete with her friends to see who could swing the highest. "The gale would have carried her away past finding, and she consented not to make the attempt then. But about seven in the evening, there was a temporary lull, and the old acrobat's heart glowed to renew her triumphs." Confidently she took her beloved rope. "Oh! the exhilaration of swinging rhythmically, now high, now low, up over the house and the village!" It will be like that, soaring with our legs over our heads, it will be airborne, flung, wrinkled, crushed, torn up, pulped, deleted, lost, dropped in the gutter all undeciphered, "those words had found their true home," wrote Assia Djebar of the love letter stolen from her purse by a begging woman, "they had fallen into the hands of that illiterate woman who disappeared," so writing will go astray, awry, it will be mislaid, it will blow to pieces, it will belong to every gesture we can make. *Transient. Transitive.* "The blue of heaven is suddenly limitless."

LIKE MADAME SAQUI, Leonora Carrington had a gray beard, which conventional people would find repulsive. "Personally," she wrote, "I find it rather gallant." England would be a matter of a few weeks, then she would embark on her lifelong dream of going to Lapland to be drawn in a vehicle by dogs, woolly dogs.

TOO SMALL? How to start? You quoted Wittgenstein: "How small a thought it takes to fill a whole life!" I confessed to you that although I had never written under a pseudonym, I was drawn to the idea of ghostwriting. Ways to be small, concealed, misplaced. Intertext. Ventriloquism. The ghostliness of collage, you wrote to me. There was something uncanny about quotation. You told me that when Rilke worked as secretary for Princess Marie von Thurn und Taxis-Hohenlohe, he used to transcribe her séances. Writing the words of phantoms, and then on the terrace he met the angel. In a storm. Voices. Voices. A star was waiting for him to notice it. A wave rolled toward him out of the distant past. I wrote that art was a communion of strangers, a séance, a private letter. Such a small thing to fill a life. I wanted to leave even my own first name behind, as a child abandons a broken toy. Through shrinking, through fading away, one becomes at last immense, yet frail—a shade. Wittgenstein took some apples out of a paper bag. He cut off the rotten pieces, thinking that these were like the bruised parts of his sentences. Thought filled all the objects. Apples were pictures of writing. I want to be the invisible in the thing. That haunts and kindles it. He wondered if there was something feminine about this way of thinking.

III

Copy

WHEN I THOUGHT of the hours of my life I had spent on a certain twenty pages of writing, which, at that point, had consumed an entire year, I felt, I wrote to you, quoting Kafka, like someone who falls and breaks both legs in the middle of the traffic of the Place de l'Opéra. It was unbearable to compare the amount of time that had passed with the little I had accomplished, especially since my life seemed to me short and crowded. TIME, I wrote. If I had more I'd be a different writer. You wrote to me of slowness and accumulation. It was true, you wrote, that time was required, but only in order for art to be ritual, process, to be about the impossibility of time. It made me think of what Claude Lévi-Strauss described as "visceral time": the rhythm of heart and lungs. This was the time of music. You quoted Bhanu Kapil, who said that when her third book took nine years to write, and went through a number of rejections and more than twenty revisions, she came to believe in duration. She even invented a chant, she said: "Re-writing is writing. Writing is re-writing." She put her hand on a grave and waited until she could feel the rhythm, faintly, of breathing. Of a cardiac output. I wanted to enter that listening stance, a position from which writing would be music. To inhabit cardiac time. It seemed true to writing that it should be a form of repetition, closer to a heartbeat than a craft. One moment like another. And perhaps, I secretly hoped, if I were meditating, I would not notice how little I had done. This secret hope was my cowardice. It proved my vulnerability to the culture of production, against which I was struggling so doggedly. I thought again of Lévi-Strauss, who was never so intimidated, he confessed, as by a morning he once spent with an elderly psychiatric patient of Paris, who told him, from among her enveloping shawls, that she felt like a rotten herring buried deep in a block of ice.

I SENT YOU the words of Alejandra Pizarnik, who said she wanted to die standing up like an axolotl drinking time in its glass cage. "The voices burn in every limb. To sink in the pinholes of light of a rainy dawn. Impossible situations. Wind, time." In the middle of a line she changed languages, writing in French now, her foreign tongue, her mirror, the language she could remember learning to write—a process that must have taken significant time. "Pas compris," she wrote. "J'ai rien compris. Pas compris un seul mot."

ROLAND BARTHES COPIED down the words of Jean-Jacques Rousseau and I copied them in my turn from Barthes's lectures on the Neutral. "From the time of my youth," Rousseau wrote, "I had set this age of forty as the terminal point for my efforts to succeed and as the one for all of my vain ambitions." A lift of the heart, already. "I was fully resolved once this age was reached that whatever situation I might be in, I would struggle no longer to get out of it and would spend the remainder of my days living from day to day without ever again concerning myself about the future." It was a special relationship to time: a certain time was marked out, the age of forty, after which *time*, in the form of the future, would no longer be a concern. It was a compromise with the clock. "The moment having come, I executed this plan without difficulty; and even though my fortune then seemed to want to take a turn for the better, I renounced it not only without regret but with actual pleasure. In releasing myself from all those lures and vain hopes, I fully gave myself up to carelessness and to the reach of mind which always constituted my most dominant pleasure and most lasting propensity." Easy to frown on his privilege here—to quit at the age of forty! The money supporting this freedom must have come from somewhere. I reminded myself that a privilege is often a good unjustly distributed. It might be what's valuable, desirable, for everyone. "I forsook the world and its pomp; I renounced all finery: no more sword, no more watch, no more white stockings, gilding, or headdress; a very simple wig, a good coarse cloth garment; and better than all that, I eradicated from my heart the cupidity and covetousness which give value to everything I was forsaking. I resigned the post I then held, for which I was in no way suited, and began to copy music at so much a page, an occupation which had always greatly appealed to me." Barthes, too, was copying, he was copying Rousseau, Tolstoy, Lao Tzu, the philosophy of Alexandre Kojève, he was noting that a good Pyrrhonian philosopher doesn't do or say anything but "lets himself be tossed by any waves whatever," which suggests a contradictory immobility in movement, or a serenity in the midst of disorder, or what's called "drift (*dérive*)." I love that, I wrote to you, the embrace of being influenced, of writing derived from some other power. For me, it's a recuperation of the word *derivative*. Is there a time of life when one becomes a copyist? When one gives up, once and for all, the attempt to determine the course of things. He was walking down the road from Ménilmontant, at about six o'clock in the evening. Suddenly a huge Great Dane was rushing down upon him. He tried to leap over it, but it knocked him to the ground. He did not feel the blow, nor the fall, nor anything of what followed until the moment he regained consciousness. Then, what he felt was *rapture*. "A delicious moment," he wrote. "I had no distinct notion of my person." Instead, there was the sky—the lofty sky, not clear yet still immeasurably lofty, with gray clouds gliding slowly across it.

WE HAD BOTH been reading Roland Barthes, especially *Camera Lucida*, his book on photography, in which he introduces the terms *studium* and *punctum*. *Studium* is the message of the photograph, its genre, its way of participating in a symbolic system. *Punctum*, on the other hand, is the incidental detail that seizes a viewer: "that accident which pricks me (but also bruises me, is poignant to me)." If the passage from Rousseau were a photograph, we could say the *studium* is the writer's retreat from society. The *punctum*, for me, is made up of two casual, radiant phrases: *a very simple wig* and *to copy music at so much a page*.

"TO BE A copyist of beloved things must be the best occupation," wrote Sarah Lehrer-Graiwer, clicking *duplicate* on a pdf of the artist Lee Lozano's notebooks. "The hands stay busy so the mind's leash can slacken. To become transparent . . ."

YOU, TOO, you wrote, were fascinated by copyists. There were writers, you said, who wrote through reading. To become steeped in the other, filled up, like Pierre Menard, author of the *Quixote*, who, as Borges wrote, "dedicated his scruples and his sleepless nights to repeating an already extant book in an alien tongue." Of course, Pierre Menard was not a copyist. He was a true original whose work was indistinguishable from a copy. His achievement was to become another. He effaced himself. Writing of this, the word you used was *kinship*.

I REMEMBERED THAT Pierre Menard's great work remained unfinished. It still lies open, like an extended hand.

OBVIOUSLY—OR MAYBE NOT—BORGES did not write that Pierre Menard "dedicated his scruples and his sleepless nights to repeating an already extant book in an alien tongue" but rather "dedicó sus escrúpulos y vigilias a repetir en un idioma ajeno un libro preexistente." We were absorbent material, swollen with translations. Retiring figures ghosted our letters with their whispered names, Dorothy S. Blair, Kate Briggs, Lydia Davis, Betsy Wing, whose occupation was to copy music at so much a page, or more precisely, à copier de la musique à tant la page, who transcribed texts that passed through them like a transparent sheet, or more precisely, as Enrique Vila-Matas wrote in his homage to copyists, *Bartleby & Co.*, "como una lámina transparente," or even more precisely—since Vila-Matas was copying Roberto Calasso—"come una lastra trasparente." There was a time when I wanted to hunt down all the clerks and scriveners who contributed to making my copies possible— not only to do the easy work of noting the translators' names in my English-language library but to discover, for example, whether Vila-Matas had read Marguerite

Duras in French and translated her himself, or whether some other French-to-Spanish translator had enabled him to transform "écrire c'est aussi ne pas parler" into "escribir también es no hablar." I gave up on this idea very quickly. I was too deep inside the brothel-museum, inside Baudelaire's dream as I had read it in Calasso's *La Folie Baudelaire*, where the vast galleries were lined with obscene pictures. For if, as Calasso wrote, the history of literature can be seen as a sinuous garland of plagiarism, or rather una sinuosa ghirlanda di plagi, it is assuredly also a sinuous garland of translation, a history of creatures as strange as those colorful birds with lively eyes, or sometimes halves of birds, metà di uccelli, moitiés d'oiseaux, wrote Baudelaire, depicted in drawings, miniatures, and photographs on the walls of that house that was both a bordello and a place of progress and science. Among the pictures of birds and half-birds hung images of amorphous beings, bizarre, monstrous, bizzarri, mostruosi, bizarres, monstrueux, he wrote, like so many aerolites, each marked with a note: "*The girl such and such, aged . . . brought forth this fetus in the year such and such.*" Surely these were the mutants, the ones in whom copying had failed, the bad translations. One of them was still alive. His face was pleasing, molto brunito, d'une couleur orientale. He was encumbered by something blackish, like a huge snake, that grew out of his head. It wound about his limbs, a leaden garland. Translation is so uncanny, I wrote to you, recalling my favorite moment from Tayeb Salih's *Season of Migration to the North*, when the narrator, drinking with friends in his remote village in Sudan, suddenly hears a strange man reciting English poetry. The poem is "Antwerp," by Ford Madox Hueffer, who changed his name shortly after he wrote it, translating himself into Ford Madox Ford. "This is Charing Cross Station, the hour's past one, / There was a faint light, / There was a great pain." This was how I first read the poem, in the English version of Salih's novel. But in fact, it's not really the English poem, I wrote to you, it's a back-translation from Arabic, an eerie double of its source. In "Antwerp," the light is not "faint," but "very little." The pain is not "great," but "so much." And in the novel, the sound of the poem creates a jolt of terror. "All of a sudden," Salih wrote, "there came to me the ghastly, nightmarish feeling that we—the men grouped together in that room—were not a reality but merely some illusion." إنما و هماً من الأوهام. It was as if an afreet had appeared before him, his eyes shooting out flames, his sad body staggering in its inky coils. Horror of the brothel-museum, vertigo and pleasure. I wandered there, my eyes dreamy and listless, حالمتين ناعستين, drowned in a dull reverberation that seemed to have no source. Écrire c'est aussi ne pas parler. It is to hush. Es aullar sin ruido.

"HOW, INDEED," ASKS Abdelfattah Kilito in *The Author and His Doubles*, "can one speak of bilingualism without citing, evoking, and invoking animals? Behind every articulation of language lies an inarticulate cry." It was in this book that I read the story I sent you, about how, in the classical period of Arabic literature, a poet might give another some lines of verse as a gift, and the poet who received the lines would claim to have composed them. So I might write a book, for example, in your style, and you would publish it under your own name. Marvelous generosity, duplicity, and cunning: an act with the quality of a fairy tale. "The serpent has a forked, black tongue," wrote al-Jahiz in *The Book of Animals*. "Someone has claimed that serpents have two tongues, but I believe this to be an error. Rather, I think that he saw the two ends of the tongue and decided there were two separate tongues."

"CAN ONE—or at least could one ever—begin to write without taking oneself for another?" asked Roland Barthes. He dreamed of copying André Gide—not only his works but his practices, his way of strolling through the world, a notebook in his pocket and a phrase in his head. Reading this, I saw copying as the foundation of all animal societies. Imitation makes community. It is an affectionate art. Oh, if only he could have become André Gide, thought Barthes, dear Gide, the way he imagined him traveling by train, reading his classics and writing his notebooks in the dining car, or better yet, the way he actually saw him, one day in 1939, in the gloom of the Brasserie Lutétia, eating a pear and reading a book!

YOU WONDERED IF a book could be a *source file*. Was this, I asked, a way for the book to be everything and never stop? Or to stop, as everything has to stop eventually, but never conclude. To extend the passion of the collector, the reading writer. Around this time, I published an essay about Mieko Kanai. When she read it, Kanai compared it to shiritori, a traditional Japanese game. "When someone says a word, we need to say the next word that starts with the last letter of the mentioned word." It was the way I wanted to write. I wished to be under the influence. Porousness, I wrote. Vulnerability to literature. What Roland Barthes called "the essential sting." You were reading Hervé Guibert, who wrote: "I often pursue the things that Barthes indicates." And Mieko Kanai was pursuing the things that Barthes indicates, she was writing, "a leather belt, with a rose stuck in it, worn above the waist," she was copying, "a cotton dress with red and white checks," perhaps with the happiness of a child at play or a strange person gathering objects, "gauze, organza, voile, and cotton muslin, summer is here," she wrote, and she found that she was completely inside the room, where everything visible was tinged with blue, the foreground featuring a bed or divan with a matching rounded cushion. Sometimes it felt as if we were all, the living and the dead, involved in an immense game of shiritori. We were all inside the room with the blue curtains, so soft and transparent that they let in the light while shutting out the sun's strongest rays. The brilliance of the light stained the upper section of the curtains like a flame that consumed, and thus entered, the woven fabric. "I simply want to say how much I love," Kanai wrote. Her fingers drenched in light. It was a bright room.

WHAT DID IT mean that we so often found ourselves reading the same writer at the same time? Were these connections necessary, you wondered, or did we perceive them only because we were unusually sensitive to a sort of dread and ecstasy in the landscape? "So she was considering in her own mind," wrote Lewis Carroll, "(as well as she could, for the hot day made her feel very sleepy and stupid), whether the pleasure of making a daisy-chain would be worth the trouble of getting up and picking the daisies, when suddenly a white rabbit with pink eyes ran close by her." What draws you, what becomes your source, and why? All I knew was that I didn't want to be Alice, much less the rabbit. I wanted to be Alice's sister, who heard the story and succumbed. "The whole place around her became alive with the strange creatures of her little sister's dream."

AT TIMES THE connections were so strong, they warped time. When she first read Barthes's *Camera Lucida*, Kanai felt as if she had read it before because it so closely resembled one of her own stories. Surely, she thought, she had written this story after reading Barthes. Yet that was impossible, as her story had been published years before *Camera Lucida*. There were sources we copied, and there was also another kind of repetition, one that seemed to well up out of the ground. Opening Jack Kerouac's *On the Road* for the first time, I read: "I told Dean that when I was a kid and rode in cars I used to imagine I held a big scythe in my hand and cut down all the trees and posts and even sliced every hill that zoomed past the window. 'Yes! Yes!' yelled Dean. 'I used to do it too only different scythe—tell you why. Driving across the West with the long stretches my scythe had to be immeasurably longer and it had to curve over distant mountains, slicing off their tops, and reach another level to get at further mountains and at the same time clip off every post along the road, regular throbbing poles.'" I read, in the first volume of Karl Ove Knausgaard's *My Struggle*, "Another fantasy I had at that time was that there were two enormous saw blades sticking out from the side of the car, chopping off everything as we drove past. Trees and streetlamps, houses and outhouses, but also people and animals. If someone was waiting for a bus they would be sliced through the middle, their top half falling like a felled tree, leaving feet and waist standing and the wound bleeding." I read, in a story I'd published before reading Kerouac or Knausgaard, "I remember when I was a kid, on long car trips, I'd imagine a giant saw was attached to my side of the car. The saw could cut through anything. It sliced fences, it sliced trees. The fences gave a swift groan and exposed the hollow insides of their poles. The trees went *snick* and fell over with juicy ease, the tops of the stumps left gleaming moist and pale, like a wound before the blood comes." Sometimes the connections warped identity. Reading Kerouac and Knausgaard, I could easily have interpreted these scenes as phallic fantasies of conquest, so was the same true for me? "I was leveling the whole country from my seat in the back of the car. I don't know why it gave me so much pleasure."

IDENTITY AS a shiver. You sent me these lines from Borges: "I always stood in fear of mirrors. When I was a little boy, there was something awful at my house. In my room we had three full-length mirrors. Then also the furniture was of mahogany, and that made a kind of dark mirror, like the mirror to be found in St. Paul's epistle. I stood in fear of them, but being a child I did not dare say anything."

HOW TO CHANNEL these shocks that seemed to come from a parallel universe? I thought of trying to work through science fiction, through images of the automaton, the body snatcher, the zombie. Yet I had already learned, as a writer of fantasies, a *genre writer*, as people said, that eventually, in writing fantasy and science fiction, one runs smack up against the problem of the code. The code is the structure demanded by the genre: what makes a work recognizable as science fiction, thriller, or romance. It's a repetition—a *stereotype*, as my friend John put it, explaining to me that this term had its origin in printmaking. These genres are literature's sweatshops. We who toil there are mass-producing prints. That's why it's fair to describe us as *genre writers*: it doesn't mean other writers don't have genre but that we *write genre* in a way others don't. We write genre instead of books. I had begun to feel hampered by these codes, and to despair of subverting them, although I still loved fantasy and science fiction, as you loved your paperback romances, you told me, with a love tinged with shame: *this yellowed form we're not supposed to collect*. I couldn't work out where the *copy* met the *essential sting*, or how the *stereotype* could provoke a *punctum*. The *punctum* of genre novels, for me, wasn't even lodged in their pages but in the sticky feel of their garish covers. The idea of writing a book that would capture that feeling seemed not only utterly beyond my powers but also stupid. Why write a book to generate something that could be had for nothing on the discard shelf of any municipal library? It was at this time that I learned that my other favorite genre, travel writing, was considered "a second-rate literary form," just like fantasy and science fiction, only for different reasons. Travel writing, wrote Sara Steinert Borella, is "a problem for academic studies" because it's too dependent on "contingent events, what happened to happen." So in one of the literatures I felt defined my sensibility as a writer, the author exerted too much control, copying a code, and in the other the author didn't exert enough but faded away, retiring, becoming merely a means for recording random events. One of these genres was too far from life and the other was too close. One was a copy machine and the other was a camera. Maybe, you wrote, the space in between was a rich place to be writing. To be the Bartleby is to be the alien.

I HAD OPPORTUNITIES. I was invited to write a "diverse story"—something with women in it, the email suggested, or the desert. I said many things, and people requested that I repeat only certain ones. "Everything I achieve and accomplish brings with it obligations," said Robert Walser, purchasing a ticket at the window. "My activity is superior to me." He vaulted into the train. When it stopped, he rushed headlong into the house of a small-town merchant to partake of four o'clock tea, all the while behaving in a polite, well-mannered, and good-natured way, as though he'd never been anything other than an upright, reliable, skillful, serviceable inhabitant of the district. There is something hollow about the reproduction of the self. Thinking again of the words of M. NourbeSe Philip, I thought it must be the resistance to codes of language in avant-garde poetry that enabled it to prove a writer's humanity. It must be the slippery, subversive character of avant-garde poetry, its attacks on habit, and what Édouard Glissant might have called its *opacity*, that made it a powerful tool for writers of color who wished to show they were human beings, superior to their activity. What, then, was the purpose of genre writing for a writer of color? To prove she was a good copyist, upright, reliable, skillful, and serviceable? To confirm, again and again, her ability to produce, upon demand, another story set in the Sahara? I shrank from this. I began to turn down the perfect invitations. Questions remained with me: the question of the stereotype, of the copy, of the seductions and aches of effacement, and of the purpose, for a writer of color, of categorizing forms of writing for a writer of color.

"IF WORDS ARE to be uttered," wrote Theresa Hak Kyung Cha, "they would be from behind the partition."

I REMEMBERED Samuel R. Delany, who said that he was always being asked to speak with Octavia E. Butler, another black science fiction writer, rather than writers of his own subgenre, cyberpunk, who were not black. It put a little pang in the center of my chest. Not that he had anything against Octavia Butler, though they were such different writers. No, of course he was happy to speak with her. I thought of Ama Ata Aidoo on the plane, and the flight attendant's question: "You want to join your two friends at the back, yes?" Aidoo saw at once that it would be awkward to refuse. So yes, she would join her "friends" at the back of the plane, she would leave her seat with the white passengers for these "friends" she'd never met, these strangers, two extremely handsome Nigerian men. Of course she'd be delighted to sit with them. It was only that she felt a pang, but after all that was something that passed quite quickly. In the end, one is grateful for almost all connections, even the ones that are by-products of a death-producing structure. "Things are working out," she wrote, "towards their dazzling conclusions." The flight was arranged so that they passed the last of Africa in the dead hours of the night. It was nearly dawn when they crossed the Mediterranean. And there was this other continent, lighted up with the first streaks of glorious summer sunshine.

STUART HALL CALLED himself a political humanist and an intellectual anti-humanist. I thought this was perfect until I had to talk about writing in public. Then my humanism and anti-humanism became hopelessly confused, and I found myself ascribing motives to what I had written in a kind of trance. How does one present a coherent self? In a way, it was the problem of finding a place on a shelf in a bookstore, that is to say the problem of being sold. It was the problem of needing to be read, that is to say legible, visible, seen, discovered, purchased, and consumed. And yet, I wrote to you, it's not just that one hates being advertised, it's something deeper, I think, something that really has to do with writing. I quoted Blanchot, who wrote of "that neutral power, formless, without a destiny, which lies behind everything that is written." This power makes the writer a person without a future or a past, someone "no longer capable of belonging to time." A writer who is writing lives in visceral time. And so to be fixed in some frozen image of historical time makes one false to writing.

"EXPERIMENTS HAVE PROVED," wrote Walter Benjamin, "that a man does not recognize his own walk on the screen or his own voice on the phonograph." When she was twenty-three years old, Mieko Kanai wrote a story, but when she read it in a magazine, it seemed inconceivable to her that she had written it. And it seemed still more inconceivable to her, *in the instant that she was writing*, that she was writing it. She thought, Some other person is writing this. Reading her words, I traced a stain of light. All books are posthumous, I realized. All writing is ghostwriting.

DEAD WRITERS, HOWEVER——THOSE who are no longer writing—they can be historical. They are at home in the past. Maybe to be fixed in time as a living writer is, in some way, to be killed, to suffer a kind of death.

AND WHY RECORD these notes, which, by the time they are written, will have been written by someone who no longer exists? What I was writing, I thought, was simply what I wanted to keep. So as not to forget. So that, when I opened my book, I could return.

"SLEPT, AWOKE, slept, awoke," wrote Kafka, "miserable life." The thought of such an existence frightened me,
and at the same time there was something vivid about its
arid atmosphere, its multiplicity and spareness. To write:
When I think about it, I must say that my education has
done me great harm in some respects. Often I think it
over and then I always have to say that my education
has done me great harm in some ways. Often I think it
over and give my thoughts free rein, without interfering,
and always, no matter how I turn or twist it, I come to
the conclusion that in some respects my education has
done me terrible harm. Often I think it over and give
my thoughts free rein, without interfering, but I always
come to the conclusion that my education has spoiled me
more than I can understand. I often think it over and
give my thoughts free rein, without interfering, but I always come to the same conclusion: that my education
has spoiled me more than all the people I know and more
than I can conceive. I almost quoted his diary to you,
but, in the end, did not: "When I look back like this I

don't know at all whether there have been any nights, everything looks to me, can you imagine, like one day without any mornings, afternoons and evenings, even without any differences in light."

IMAGINE, I WROTE, a series of blocks, illuminated like windows. You were writing what you described as *little doors*. We were both drawn to the idea of the sequence, the line of works, like a procession of images cast onto a screen. Rilke in Vienna, lecturing on Rodin by the light of a magic lantern. It was, of course, a way of remaining incomplete. The series of small books suggests collage, I wrote to you. It's always unfinished. The poet as lamplighter, kindling flames down an endless street. Fantasy writers understand the secret process embedded here, which is why the genre is almost defined by the series, the sequel, the cycle: the spaces between the streetlamps make the world. The world doesn't dwell in the poet's light but in the obscure distances made palpable at its edge. The first volume of a fantasy establishes nothing. Only when the second volume is published does the make-believe world become real, as the reader realizes it's continued, an immeasurable history has been going on in the darkness, over *there*. Rilke onstage, describing Rodin's sculptures: "The stones preserve, even in the midst of the day, that mysterious shimmer which white things exhale in the twilight. This radiance is not the result of the vibrant quality of the points of contact alone, but is due in part to the flat ribbands of stone that lie between the figures like small bridges which connect one form with the other." Only with fragments can you make a universe; this is what we call *worldbuilding*. And how I wanted always to stand on the small bridge, on one of those ribbands of stone that links the forms. To gather the light like a vase that gently and continuously overflows.

AMONG THE FORMS of repetition, there must be one that forces a person to appear again and again in the same garb, and this makes a deadly feeling. And there must be another form of repetition in which a child imitates a rabbit, and this makes a lively feeling. There must also be a form of repetition in which the artist Hokusai draws over two hundred lions. This is ecstatic. "I know that I have mentioned this already," Clarice Lispector wrote, "but I am repeating it out of my zest for happiness: I want the same thing over and over again."

SUSAN RUBIN SULEIMAN wrote that Hélène Cixous worked on the same subjects over and over until they became "decanted." I loved this idea of writing as distillation, a chemical process. Cixous wrote that she wanted to be a painter. She wanted, like Monet, to paint the cathedral twenty-six times, to make a sheaf of paintings, a herd, a flock, a tribe. She wanted to paint the cathedral until she saw it in all its lights. "My sleep was filled with nightmares," she wrote, quoting Monet. "The cathedral fell down on top of me, it appeared either blue, pink or yellow." She quoted Hokusai: "I continue to draw hoping for a peaceful day." She quoted Jean Genet, who wrote of Rembrandt that he began by gilding, by covering surfaces with gold, and then he burned the gold, consumed it, in order to attain the gold-ash with which he painted his last paintings. Another process from the chemist's lab: a burning away. "Art is not purity," Lispector wrote, "it is purification." I wrote to you that this reminded me of religious language: the Isaac Watts hymn about purifying the heart until it became perfume. And it was also, I wrote, the Sufi ideal of polishing the heart until its

brightness reflected only the divine. So for me this becomes a question of writing, I wrote. How do you purify,
how do you polish? (The repetitive motion of polishing.)
How to annihilate the self. To reach the Sufi *fanaa‘*: the
void. Monet in his fury burning thirty canvases. "It is
only at the end of a superhuman human-going-to-the-
depths-of-the-fathoming-of-life-and-back that one will
be able to cease gilding everything," wrote Cixous. "And
then one can begin to adore."

"WHAT DO COPYISTS dream of?" asked Abdelfattah Kilito. "Of rest, it seems." This reminded me of the cartoon on the wall of the copy room at work, which showed a pair of monks, one of them collapsed on top of his papers, the other announcing: "Printer's down!" Kilito recounted the story of Ibn al-Hadina, who dreamed that he died and went to Paradise, where there was no more writing. "I lay on my back, crossed my legs, and told myself that I was through with copying. But I woke up and found my pen in my hand and the copy-sheets before me."

WHAT WAS THE goal of this endless quest? I sent you some lines from Blanchot. "Is Cézanne's concern to express himself, to give to art, that is, one more artist? He 'swore to die painting.' Was that just in order to live on? Does he sacrifice himself in this passion which knows no happiness simply so that his paintings might give form to the singular weather of his soul?" Blanchot knew better than that. This went far beyond self-expression. There is a tender empiricism that makes itself inwardly identical with the object. He felt this with a certainty that did not cease to hurt. "This much no one can doubt: what he seeks has only one name. Painting."

IV

Night

ANNIHILATE THE SELF, we wrote to one another. I don't know how many times. Annihilate the self. It wasn't about death, mysticism, or equilibrium, it was about reinventing oneself as a writer. Withdrawal was chrysalis. How to grow a completely different lung, for another breath. "My work was only created by *elimination*," wrote Mallarmé, "and every truth established born only of the loss of an impression which, having sparkled, burnt itself out and allowed me, thanks to the timbres it emitted, to go deeper into the sensation of the Absolute Shadows." Words I typed and sent to you one night. Early December: Rilke's birthday. It was the season of Absolute Shadows, the time of closing the book, snuffing the candle, and folding one's arms to lie down on the tomb. "Destruction was my Beatrice."

I SENT YOU a line by Kafka: "I need solitude for my writing; not 'like a hermit'—that wouldn't be enough—but like a dead man." Two boys were sitting on the harbor wall playing with dice. A man was reading a newspaper on the steps of the monument, resting in the shadow of a hero who was flourishing his sword on high. You told me you tried to write as if already dead. A girl filled her bucket at the fountain. A fruit seller lay beside his wares, gazing at the lake. I sent you a fragment of Stanley Cavell: "telling the accidental, anonymous, in a sense posthumous, days of my life is the making of philosophy." Through the vacant window and doors of a café one could see two men at the back drinking their wine. The proprietor was sitting at a table in front and dozing. I told you I'd found a solution to the problem of authorship: write for posthumous publication. Once, I'd thought I was doing this, that my first book would never be published. At that time, never being published seemed a very real possibility. Of course I can't be unpublished now. But I could decide not to publish again. Or try somehow to achieve a posthumous mode of writing. The bark was silently making for the little harbor, as if borne by invisible means over the water. "Anyone who cannot cope with life while he is alive," Kafka wrote, "needs one hand to ward off a little his despair over his fate . . . but with his other hand he can jot down what he sees among the ruins, for he sees different and more things than the others." A man in a blue blouse climbed ashore and drew the rope through a ring. Behind the boatman two other men in dark coats with silver buttons carried a bier, on which, beneath a great flower-patterned fringed silk cloth, a man was apparently lying: dead in his own life-time, the real survivor.

"IF I HAVE to die," wrote Kanai, "I would've liked to die in my nest." The posthumous mode was another way of imagining the book without an end. The posthumously published writer has died within her book. She has escaped. She will not be pried out of the book that is her nest. No, unfortunately, she is not available for interviews. However, on the bright side, she doesn't mind being built up into some historical figure. Please do what you like with her nest. She requires no additional transformation now. My dream image: a patchwork of tiny bones.

"LIKE A LITTLE work of art," said Friedrich Schlegel, his right hand on his heart, his left on his forehead, "a fragment must be totally detached from the surrounding world and closed in on itself like a hedgehog." It was the dream of withdrawal, the fantasy of the nest. One would not only collect the most precious items in a shoebox, one would also get inside the box. There, among the notes, the scribbled fragments, one would live as in that forgotten nook at the end of a narrow, dark corridor, where, Benjamin recalled, between a librairie en solde, in which masses of books were stacked in dusty tied-up bundles, and a shop selling only buttons (mother-of-pearl, and the kind that in Paris is called *de fantaisie*), he discovered a sort of salon. "On the pale-colored wallpaper full of figures and busts shone a gas lamp. By its light, an old woman sat reading. They say she has been there alone for years." Alone for years. As if released. "Occasionally," Rilke wrote, "I pass by little shops—in the rue de Seine, for example. Dealers in antiques or small second-hand booksellers or vendors of engravings with overcrowded windows. No one ever enters their shops; they apparently do no business. But if one looks in, they are sitting there, sitting and reading, without a care; they take no thought for the morrow, are not anxious about any success, have a dog that sits before them, all good-nature, or a cat that makes the silence still greater by gliding along the rows of books, as if it were rubbing the names off their backs."

"AH," HE WROTE, "if that were enough: sometimes I would like to buy such a full shop-window for myself and to sit down behind it with a dog for twenty years." For weeks now he had been living in a tent deep in the forest of Argilly, declaring that for his solace he must hear the stags belling in the night.

YOU TOLD ME Barthes had written that *punctum* extends from the same Latin root as *punctuation*. He wakened in himself the rumpled softness of her crêpe de Chine. What is the relationship of the *punctum* to language? you asked. To silence? Is it where language ends? And the perfume of her rice powder. Every time I typed *punctum* the autocorrect software altered it to *puncture*. How overwhelming it would be to create an album made up of this. Pure puncture, like a line of music soundless on the page, abstract and wounding. I remembered Bhanu Kapil writing at the end of *Schizophrene*, "As I removed the second period that came at the end of each sentence, a method of punctuation learned in England, I understood that I was reversing a line of black dots." These dots, she explained, became the matter of an anti-colonial novel. All at once I saw the coloniality of *rice powder* and *crêpe de Chine*, their exotic and brutal sumptuousness. I felt this as puncture, as a silence, something that could not be said and cried out to be said. I thought of Edward Said's theory of contrapuntal reading, a method that takes in both what is said and what is *forcibly excluded*, both imperialism and resistance, both Barthes's mood and the commodities that conjure that mood, both the sentence and the silence that follows. The line of black dots. Punctus contra punctum. Point against point. Note against note. One would read as if in time to a metronome. My problem with contrapuntal reading was that it suggested the possibility of harmony, of a stable set of relations. After all, listening to Mozart is very easy and pleasurable, but this is not the case with contrapuntal reading, in which, once the silence of the oppressed has been released, it obliterates the melody of the text. Instead of producing music, one point cancels the other out. Yet I remained a person who wished to have everything. Was it worth it, in this condition, to go on writing? "To puncture to scratch to imprint," wrote Theresa Hak Kyung Cha. "Expel. Ne te cache pas. Révèle-toi."

I WANTED it all. Every kind of art for every kind of person. But some people, I saw, must not *annihilate the self.* Certain bodies by virtue of being these bodies are tasked with the care of the world. They represent whole tribes. For them, there is no nest. These, the exemplars, will be denied all relief from vigilance. They will not be granted a moment of abstraction.

TO WANT, to see, to write it all. "Intensity," Octavia E. Butler wrote. The walls were shaking. It was all hammering back and forth. "Cold or hot, hard or soft, gut-wrenching or deeply stilling," she wrote in black and then red, "utter intensity." I copied the words of Anaïs Nin into my computer: "The world is too small. I get tired of playing the guitar, of knitting, and walking, and bearing children . . . I get furious at stairways, furious at doors, at walls, furious at everyday life which interferes with the continuity of ecstasy. But," she warned, "there is a martyrdom of tenseness, of fever, of living continuously like the firmament in full movement and in full effulgence." In the train once, going to Berlin where her father was to give a concert, she had such an earache that she began to weep. To want, to see, to write it all, even things that canceled each other out, required intensity, a mind worked up to a raging pressure. There was the threat of martyrdom. I thought of Clarice Lispector, who said, "I'd like to write a story full of all the instants, but that would suffocate even the protagonist." I felt the danger of suffocation, of shorting myself out, of some kind of collapse, like that of the girl on the train, moaning from her earache. Is there a place where writing crosses into its opposite? If you don't stop crying and go to sleep, her father said, I'll beat you. She stuffed her head under the pillow so that he would not hear her sobs. She wrote: "You never saw the stars grow weary or dim. They never sleep." The train was rocking, jolting as if it might throw itself off the rails. It was *resonant*. She sobbed all the way to Berlin.

I TOLD YOU all my plans. I want to write a book that is stripped down to almost nothing, like a screenplay, about being exposed to an alien influence. I want to write a decadent anachronistic book. I want to write a vulgar political book—one that's very mean. I want to do nothing but learn foreign languages. I want to be like the other moms at the soccer game, who—I imagine snobbishly—are not writers.

I SENT YOU the words of Mieko Kanai: "If there is one idea that obsesses me, it is, How can I stop writing?"

"UNTIL TODAY," Clarice Lispector wrote, "I did not realize that you can live without writing. Little by little the thought dawned upon me: Who knows? Perhaps I, too, might be able to live without writing." Certainly, if she could finish her account, she would go, that very day, to eat and dance at the Top-Bambino. She mightily needed to have a good time and distract herself. She'd eat crevettes and not worry about how many. Like us, she was in search of a writing that was more like living. "If only I could write by carving on wood or stroking a child's hair or strolling through the countryside," she wrote, selecting the blue dress that made her look a little thinner, "I should never have embarked upon the path of words."

THE WRITING VOICE must go, must disappear. Enrique Vila-Matas wrote: "I have only existed, the voice says, if talk of me can be talk of life. It says it is eclipsing itself, it is going, to end here would be perfect, but it wonders if this is desirable. And it answers itself that it is, that to finish here would be marvelous, perfect, whoever it is, wherever it is."

AND HOW WONDERFUL it would be, I thought, to open up completely, to not be writing this book anymore. Perhaps the goal of this book has been to reach a state of suspension from which what was once writing will pulse like a dark star.

ASSIA DJEBAR: "But my sole ambition in writing is constantly to travel to fresh pastures and replenish my waterskins with an inexhaustible silence." To go to the depths. Somehow I kept on writing in the notebooks, because I still wanted to be over there.

"EVERY GREAT SPIRIT carries on in his life two works,"
wrote Victor Hugo, "the work of the living person and
the work of the phantom . . . Whereas the living man
performs the first work, the pensive phantom—at night,
amid the universal silence—awakes within the man. O
terror!" Terror, the hounds and the foxes yelping, darkness everywhere, nature shuddering, yet I wanted to
be the phantom awake in the night. I said, I will be the
writer-specter. "Without understanding the reason,"
wrote Anna Kavan, "I knew that I had to keep the day
unimportant." She had to keep the day world from becoming real. All day she waited for the night. She grew
taller and thinner, her face chalk-white and haggard, her
hair curled into a stiff sacrificial crown. Even her dress
changed color, turning red-black, so that she stood like a
dark pillar before the blank window. Why, why do this?
Didn't it sometimes seem to you as if life could have been
easier? Yet she *had to* establish reality in another place.
Words took fright, sentences shivered, the windowpane
grew dim, the lamp was afraid, "Get up! Up!" cried the
specter, "there is a great wind abroad," and she struck

out, fearing to drown in so black a sea, she thrashed
about desperately in pursuit of the images that appeared,
transparent as the shadows of icicles, incorporated in the
night-plasma, no sound, no motion, nothing to indicate
either sea or land, and it was the moment she longed for,
the moment of going home to her night world.

"O NIGHT without objects," Rilke wrote. In the evenings, when darkness fell, there were of course only lights for the whole household, common lights. But the two candles, quite early in the new darkness, with which everything began again, those he had to himself. They stood in their low double sconce, shining peacefully through the small, oval shade of tulle painted with roses, which had to be slid down from time to time. There was nothing disturbing in that; for one thing, he was in absolutely no hurry, and then it would so happen that he had to look up and reflect, when he was writing at a letter or in the diary which had been begun once long ago in an entirely different hand, timorous and beautiful.

"ALL NIGHT LONG I make the night," Alejandra Pizarnik wrote. "All night long I write. Word by word I am writing the night."

AS FOR ME, I had gone in search of a writing cure, and I found these three solutions: the box, the copy, and the night. The box was a way of shaping, the copy was a way of working, and the night was the world where everything took place. "The burning electric light," wrote Kafka, "the silent house, the darkness outside, the last waking moments, they give me the right to write, even if it be only the most miserable stuff," and he took this right, he took it hurriedly, because that was the person he was. In this night world, which was writing, one could feel that, as Clarice Lispector wrote, *I* is only a word people form with their lips when answering the telephone, one could feel that, as Leonora Carrington wrote, "*I am* may have been a dishonest invention meaning multitude," one could sense quite clearly that, as she also wrote, "If I am my thoughts, then I could be anything from chicken soup to a pair of scissors, a crocodile, a corpse, a leopard or a pint of beer," and it wasn't an escape from the world but rather an entering in, it was talk of life, it was one of those mornings Rilke wrote of, made of a million tiny insuppressible movements, when objects vibrate into one another and out into the air, there is no main object in the garden, everything is everywhere diffused, and one would have to be in everything in order to miss nothing.

"I JUST NEED to be able to look without having the color of my eyes matter," Clarice Lispector wrote. "I need to get rid of myself to be able to see." She felt that there was something between herself and everything around her, as if she were one of those people with a white film covering their eyes. She felt terribly that she needed to say that this veil was precisely her desire to work and to see too much. And yet—such perfume! It was Sunday morning. "And I also have no name, and that is my name. And because I depersonalize to the point of having no name, I shall answer every time someone says: me."

AND SO WHAT I sought was not, as I'd written to you, a *project of nothing* but a *project of everything*. Or, rather, it was both at once. It was a night world that trembled with a vibrant morning. It was a close and friendly dissolution. It was a withdrawal that made one open to every passing current of air, touched by the gleam of every instant. It was the rhythm of heart and lungs, a strange and common language. It was music. It was contrapuntal writing.

"MY FINAL WORD was *I*," Alejandra Pizarnik wrote, "but by this I meant the luminous dawn."

AND I'VE WRITTEN to you as Schlegel wrote to Novalis. For Schlegel declared that he spoke only to those who were already facing the dawn. To Novalis he wrote, "Every doctrine of the eternal Orient belongs to all artists. I name you instead of all the others."

"SO LONG AS writing, including the act of not writing, is writing," wrote Mieko Kanai, "then perhaps inevitably, writing is my fate." It was still early morning, and the smell of the dust that had sunk into the earth and gravel during the night mingled with the exhalations of the trees and vegetation, leaving a sweetness in the cool dawn atmosphere. Expanding her slightly painful rib cage—using the muscles that were stretched around the ribs—she breathed the sweetness in, and the pain, turning into particles, was drawn with it into the depths of her lungs.

ANNIHILATE THE SELF, we wrote, we chanted to each other. All we wanted was to be born.

I CAN NEVER understand, I wrote to you, what form a work should take. It's like everything has to be written not only from the beginning of the work but actually from the beginning of all writing, as if nothing's ever been written before, as if I've never read anything. I copied into my notebook the words of Sergio Pitol: "Does each book, then, have to start from zero?" And Rilke: "At the onset of every work, you must re-create that primal innocence, you must return to that ingenuous place where the Angel found you." It was night, it was winter, he was freezing, he was writing, "you must seek through the brambles for the bed in which you then slept; this time you won't sleep: you will pray, wail— anything; if the Angel condescends to come, it will be because you have persuaded him, not with your tears, but by your humble decision always to start afresh—*to be a beginner!*" Always to start, never to end, my friend. "She says to herself if she were able to write she could continue to live," wrote Theresa Hak Kyung Cha. "Says to herself if she would write without ceasing. To herself if by writing she could abolish real time. She would live."

It was everything we wanted. It was the luminous dawn. It was the unwritten, never-to-be-written, never-ending, always-beginning book. It was the book that left nothing behind, neither its speed nor its sickness, neither its night world nor its morning, neither its body nor its phantom, neither its pleasure nor its resistance nor its joy nor its complaint nor its critique nor its lament nor its resentment nor its shame nor its spontaneous things that were happening everywhere now when, having written all night, we were as agreeably tired as after a long walk over the fields of Ulsgaard, and we realized, holding hands, that if this was a book without an end, then there was nothing to prevent us from beginning right here, in the cool freshness, among the many voices that made a mosaic of most convincing life, where the shadows were clear and the sun a spiritual transparency, for if writing never ends, then to start right here is altogether marvelous, perfect, whoever it is, wherever it is.

ACKNOWLEDGMENTS

I want to thank the friends, supporters, and admired writers and artists who inspired and fostered this project. Thank you, Ashon Crawley, John Jennings, K'eguro Macharia, and Rosalind Palermo Stevenson for your words and reading suggestions. Thanks to my agent, Sally Harding, and my editor, Mensah Demary, for believing in this book and guiding it to publication with such care. To my research assistant, Nick Handakas, thanks for your indispensable help with the notes. Thank you, Cecilia Flores, Wah-Ming Chang, and Elana Rosenthal for your assistance, edits, and expert fact-checking. Thank you, Kumiko Kanai, for permission to use *The Letter from Akiko* on the cover of this book; thanks to Mieko Kanai and Mina Kitahara for permission to quote your conversation reported in an email to me; and thank you, Hiroki Yamamoto, for your kind efforts in facilitating the permissions process. To Keith Miller, thanks for your enthusiasm and encouragement. To Kate Zambreno, essential interlocutor for many years now, I send my gratitude for our ongoing conversation about writing, and my love.

NOTE ON METHOD

Opacities is a series of encounters in literature. Writers appear in this book as they do on the page. Descriptions of writers traveling, eating, and so on are drawn from their letters, diaries, essays, poetry, and fiction. Within this space, writers become their characters: Madame Bovary is Flaubert. Sometimes writers slide into one another's work, as when Mieko Kanai copies Roland Barthes or Barthes channels Tolstoy. I have used allusion, paraphrase, and direct quotation of sources that can be found in the notes below. This layering of voices is the best means I have found of answering the question: Who are you when you write?

NOTES

EPIGRAPH

xi Édouard Glissant, *Poétique de la relation* (Paris: Gallimard, 1990), 209.

I: TONIC

3 "I'm beginning a new book...": Hervé Guibert, *To the Friend Who Did Not Save My Life*, trans. Linda Coverdale (Los Angeles: Semiotext(e), 2020), 18.

3 The Pillow Book of Sei Shōnagon in the country: Hervé Guibert, *The Gangsters*, trans. Iain White (London: Serpent's Tail, 1991), 17.

3 Shivering with cold . . . salty biscuit: ibid., 46.

3 "(Living with a book . . .)": Hervé Guibert, *The Mausoleum of Lovers: Journals 1976–1991*, trans. Nathanaël (New York: Nightboat Books, 2014), 537.

5 "This is what is diabolical...": Gustave Flaubert, letter to Louise Colet, trans. Eugenio Donato, in Donato, "A Mere Labyrinth of Letters/Flaubert and the Quest for Fiction/A Montage," *MLN* 89, 6 (1974): 890.

5 cooling . . . andirons: Gustave Flaubert, *Madame Bovary*, trans. Francis Steegmuller (New York: Random House, 1957), 25–26.

5 obsessive bells, and rain: Aimé Césaire, *Notebook of a*

Return to the Native Land, trans. Clayton Eshleman and Annette Smith (Middletown, CT: Wesleyan University Press, 2001), 10.

8 shifting his existence and his writing out of people's sight: Johann Wolfgang von Goethe, quoted in Rüdiger Safranski, *Goethe: Life as a Work of Art*, trans. David Dollenmayer (New York: Liveright, 2017), 273.

8 the half-obliterated groaning of the spirits: Johann Wolfgang von Goethe, *The Sorrows of Young Werther*, trans. Bayard Quincy Morgan (London: Alma Classics, 2015), 86.

8 tried to hide his poems . . . happy cry: Rainer Maria Rilke, *The Notebooks of Malte Laurids Brigge*, trans. M. D. Herter Norman (New York: W. W. Norton, 1949), 197.

8 "Only an angel . . . nothing but you": ibid., 197.

11 "My name . . .": Alejandra Pizarnik, *Extracting the Stone of Madness: Poems 1962–1972*, trans. Yvette Siegert (New York: New Directions, 2016), 103.

11 "Give up . . .": Édouard Glissant, *Poetics of Relation*, trans. Betsy Wing (Ann Arbor: University of Michigan Press, 1997), 190.

13 no identity: John Keats, *Selected Letters* (Penguin Classics, 2015), 263.

13 nomads and immigrants: Gilles Deleuze and Félix Guattari, *Kafka: Toward a Minor Literature*, trans. Dana Polan (Minneapolis: University of Minnesota Press, 1986), 19.

13 the whole field of desire and history . . . escape: Dana Polan, "Translator's Introduction" in Deleuze and Guattari, *Kafka: Toward a Minor Literature*, xxiii.

13 "This is my farewell": Hilton Als, *White Girls* (San Francisco: McSweeney's, 2013), 136.

13 Joni Mitchell's autobiography: ibid., 11.

15 "Here we are on Wuthering Heights": ibid., 42.

16 "Writing letters . . .": Franz Kafka, *Letters to Milena*, trans. Phillip Boehm (New York: Schocken Books, 1990), 230.

18 She entered between the two white columns . . . 6:35 p.m.: Theresa Hak Kyung Cha, *Dictee* (Berkeley: University of California Press, 2001), 94.

18 "you are the audience . . .": Theresa Hak Kyung Cha, *Audience Distant Relative* (Berkeley, CA: Berkeley Art Museum, 1977), 3. Handmade artist book.

18 She handed her ticket . . . half a step: Cha, *Dictee*, 94.

18 "as if a distant relative . . .": Cha, *Audience Distant Relative*, 3.

19 "My people . . .": Franz Kafka, quoted in Hannah Arendt, "Walter Benjamin: 1892–1940," in Walter Benjamin, *Illuminations*, trans. Harry Zohn (New York: Schocken Books, 1968), 36.

20 "negative community . . ." Georges Bataille, quoted in Maurice Blanchot, *The Unavowable Community*, trans. Pierre Joris (Barrytown, NY: Station Hill, 1988), 24.

20 "the anonymity of the book": ibid., 24.

20 You wouldn't know . . . inmost self: Marguerite Duras, *The Malady of Death*, trans. Barbara Bray (New York: Grove Weidenfield, 1986), 1. Blanchot copies Duras in *The Unavowable Community*, 35.

20 how can loving happen . . . act of will: Duras, *The Malady of Death*, 49–50.

20 Until that night . . . touch: ibid., 17.

21 Facing . . . stranger might: ibid., 23.

22 The black sea . . . falling: ibid., 27.

22 "These notes link me . . .": Georges Bataille, quoted in Blanchot, *The Unavowable Community*, 24.

23 "Correspondence . . .": Cha, *Dictee*, 48.

24 "No poem . . .": Benjamin, *Illuminations*, 69.

24 his practice of lifting quotations . . . him alone: Arendt, "Walter Benjamin: 1892–1940," 45.

25 "(the principle of incompleteness)": Blanchot, *The Unavowable Community*, 5.

25 "In their eyes . . .": Haytham El Wardany, *Jama'at al-adab al-naqis: qisas*, trans. Robin Moger, epigraph to Youssef Rakha, *The Crocodiles*, trans. Robin Moger (New York: Seven Stories, 2014).

25 cheap latticework table . . . closed against the cold": Haytham El Wardany, *Jama'at al-adab al-naqis: qisas* (Cairo: Dar Mirit, 2003), 8. My translation.

25 The embroidered hangings . . . days: ibid., 11.

26 entangled with all the sounds of the city . . . alarms: ibid., 19–20.

26 an ocean of silence . . . absorbed: ibid., 21.

27 to begin to exist: Clarice Lispector, *The Passion According to G. H.*, trans. Ronald W. Sousa (Minneapolis: University of Minnesota Press, 1988), 15.

27 "During the time . . .": ibid., 10.

29 "Today I wrote nothing . . .": Daniil Kharms, *The Blue Notebook*, trans. Matvei Yankelevich (New York: Ugly Duckling Presse, 2004), 14.

29 "creations": Can Xue, *Five Spice Street*, trans. Karen Gernant and Chen Zeping (New Haven, CT: Yale University Press, 2009), 326.

29 repetitive, and excessively long: ibid., 326.

29 gained experience: ibid., 324.

29 "Sometimes . . .": ibid., 324–25.

29 She picked up . . . thicket: ibid., 328.

29 After the collapse . . . quiet: ibid., 324.

30 "Empathy as a theme . . .": Jim Lyons, quoted in Lisa Cohen, "Acute, Attenuated," *Animal Shelter* 4 (2016): 79.

30 NEW YORK . . . Christmas season: Jim Lyons, "A Short Film About Andy Warhol," *Esopus* 9 (2007): 9.

30 kitchen . . . steel: ibid., 11.

30 CLOSE . . . shelf: ibid., 11.

30 "Since I was a boy . . .": Jim Lyons, quoted in Amy Taubin, "Notes on 'A Short Film About Andy Warhol,'" *Esopus* 9 (2007): 16.

31 The blue light . . . channels: Lyons, "A Short Film About Andy Warhol," 11.

31 a sinuous garland of plagiarism: Roberto Calasso, *La Folie Baudelaire*, trans. Alastair McEwen (New York: Farrar, Straus and Giroux, 2012), 7.

31 Amber, sapphire . . . skin: Lyons, "A Short Film About Andy Warhol," 13.

31 "Not what's inside . . .": ibid., 13.

31 A piercing . . . stillness: ibid., 13.

31 kettle off the burner . . . teacup: ibid., 13.

32 line of moisture . . . weeping: ibid., 13.

32 "Too big? . . . How to start?": Jim Lyons, quoted in Cohen, "Acute, Attenuated," 79.

33 their claim . . . makes it take flight: Deleuze and Guattari, *Kafka: Toward a Minor Literature*, 71.

33 "The highest desire . . .": ibid., 71.

33 a peculiar rattling . . . regular: Franz Kafka, "Blumfeld, an Elderly Bachelor," trans. Tania and James Stern, in *Franz Kafka: The Complete Stories*, ed. Nahum N. Glatzer (New York: Schocken Books, 1971), 184–85.

33 "A machine . . .": Deleuze and Guattari, *Kafka: Toward a Minor Literature*, 71.

33 When one of them . . . game: Kafka, "Blumfeld, an Elderly Bachelor," 185.

34 sits in a corner . . . contagious disease: ibid., 184.

36 "Let us not . . .": Jane Austen, *Northanger Abbey* (New York: Cambridge University Press, 2006), 30.

II: BOX

39 into the dark garden: Bhanu Kapil, *Schizophrene* (New York: Nightboat Books, 2011), 1.

39 wet grid: ibid., 4.

39 Doorway . . . ruins: ibid., 59.

41 "The collector . . .": Walter Benjamin, *The Arcades Project*, trans. Howard Eiland and Kevin McLaughlin (Cambridge, MA: Harvard University Press, 1999), 205.

42 "The writing consists . . .": Walter Benjamin, quoted in Arendt, "Walter Benjamin: 1892–1940," 8.

42 the most banal . . . hour: Benjamin, *Illuminations*, 203.

42 An everyday hour . . . window: ibid., 203.

42 blind, senseless . . . love: ibid., 203.

42 "Nothing was more characteristic . . .": Arendt, "Walter Benjamin: 1892–1940," 45.

43 a Hunter . . . Rarities: Samuel Taylor Coleridge, *Coleridge on the Seventeenth Century*, ed. Roberta Florence Brinkley (Durham, NC: Duke University Press, 1955), 448.

43 a film . . . an inventory: Theo Angelopoulos, *Theo Angelopoulos: Interviews*, ed. Dan Fainaru (Jackson: University Press of Mississippi, 2001), 74, 109.

45 "all the fascination . . .": Mieko Kanai, *The Word Book*, trans. Paul McCarthy (Champaign, IL: Dalkey Archive, 2009), 11.

45 She was drinking her second coffee . . . north: ibid., 1–2.

45 "My first camera . . .": ibid., 15.

45 "The aperture . . .": ibid., 15.

46 "In fact, I thought . . .": ibid., 15.

47 "Wasn't it simply . . .": ibid., 18.

48 "for the way he chooses . . . his concern": M. John Harrison, *Parietal Games: Critical Writings by and on M. John Harrison*, ed. Mark Bould and Michelle Reid (London: Science Fiction Foundation, 2005), 147.

48 Benjamin's three stages of prose writing: Walter Benjamin, *One-Way Street*, trans. Edmund Jephcott (Cambridge, MA: Belknap, 2016), 41.

49 "Which of us, in his moments of ambition . . .": Charles Baudelaire, *Paris Spleen*, trans. Louise Varèse (New York : New Directions, 1970), 3.

49 "repetitive scraps": Ousmane Sembène, *Xala*, trans. Clive Wake (Chicago: Lawrence Hill, 1976), 26.

49 "say something about the method . . .": Benjamin, *The Arcades Project*, 456.

51 "The day I manage . . .": Clarice Lispector, "Six Letters from Clarice Lispector," trans. Ana Fletcher, *Music & Literature* 4 (2014): 26.

52 "I shall be derelict": Frantz Fanon, *Black Skin, White Masks*, trans. Charles Lam Markmann (New York: Grove Press, 1967), 12.

52 "And why don't you write? . . .": Hélène Cixous, "The Laugh of the Medusa," in *The Portable Cixous*, trans. Keith Cohen and Paula Cohen (New York: Columbia University Press, 2010), 28.

52 "like victims . . .": Antonin Artaud, *The Theater and Its Double*, trans. Mary Caroline Richards (New York: Grove Press, 1958), 13.

52 "Write without making . . .": Marguerite Duras, *Emily L.*, trans. Barbara Bray (New York: Pantheon, 1989), 112.

52 the Java Sea . . . the Natuna archipelago: ibid., 108.

52 lay down . . . dead on the deck: ibid., 109–10.

52 "One ought to eject . . .": ibid., 112.

54   "the impossibility of writing German" . . . "the impossibil-
     ity of writing" . . . "*the impossibility of not writing*": Franz
     Kafka, letter to Max Brod, in *Letters to Friends, Family,
     and Editors*, trans. Richard and Clara Winston (New York:
     Schocken Books, 1977), 289. Emphasis added.

55   the café in Berkeley . . . in 2011: Bhanu Kapil, *Ban en Ban-
     lieue* (New York: Nightboat Books, 2016), 9.

55   "I am not interested in disclosure . . .": Petra Kuppers,
     quoted in Kapil, *Ban en Banlieue*, 9.

57   "There is much I cannot tell you . . .": Clarice Lispector,
     Água Viva, trans. Stefan Tobler (New York: New Direc-
     tions, 2012), 29.

58   "The purpose of avant-garde writing . . .": M. NourbeSe
     Philip, quoted in Mg Roberts, "Displacement Is a Moment
     of Translation," interview with Maw Shein Win, *The Mar-
     gins* (Sept. 26, 2016), aaww.org/mg-roberts-displacement/.

60   "Every angel is terrifying": Rainer Maria Rilke, "The First
     Elegy," in *The Selected Poetry of Rainer Maria Rilke*, trans.
     Stephen Mitchell (New York: Vintage, 1989), 151.

60   To be the traveler . . . gentian: Rilke, "The Ninth Elegy," in
     The Selected Poetry of Rainer Maria Rilke, 199.

60   "There is a tender empiricism . . .": Johann Wolfgang von
     Goethe, *Maxims and Reflections*, trans. John McCole, quoted
     in John McCole, *Walter Benjamin and the Antinomies of Tra-
     dition* (Ithaca, NY: Cornell University Press, 1993), 132.

60   house, pitcher, fruit tree, window: Rilke, "The Ninth El-
     egy," in *The Selected Poetry of Rainer Maria Rilke*, 199.

61   an essay on Walter Benjamin by Susan Buck-Morss: Susan
     Buck-Morss, "Aesthetics and Anaesthetics: Walter Ben-
     jamin's Artwork Essay Reconsidered," *October* 62 (1992):
     3–41.

63   "If I remember correctly . . .": Leonora Carrington, *The

Hearing Trumpet (London: Routledge & Kegan Paul, 1977), 21.

66 "Each one of these sentences...": Ludwig Wittgenstein, quoted in "Translator's Introduction," *Wittgenstein's Tractatus*, trans. Daniel Kolak (Mountain View, CA: Mayfield, 1998), xi.

66 the high wall... sky: Alfred Kubin, *The Other Side*, trans. Mike Mitchell (Cambridgeshire, UK: Dedalus, 2014), 47.

66 a melancholy journey: ibid., 48.

66 enough to make a man sick: ibid., 47.

67 "one's body is most vibrant...": Can Xue, *Vertical Motion*, trans. Karen Gernant and Chen Zeping (Rochester, NY: Open Letter, 2011), 16.

67 "The artist Kubin recommends...": Franz Kafka, *The Diaries of Franz Kafka 1910–1913*, trans. Joseph Kresh (New York: Schocken Books, 1948), 67.

68 Kubin resting his foot... his trousers: ibid., 67.

68 Later, seeing... "But you are really sick!": ibid., 71.

68 "When someone is vomiting...": Marguerite Duras, *The Ravishing of Lol Stein*, trans. Richard Seaver (New York: Pantheon, 1986), 164.

69 to "wink" or "radiate": Bruno Schulz, letter to *Wiadomości Literackie*, in Jerzy Ficowski, *Regions of the Great Heresy: Bruno Schulz, a Biographical Portrait*, trans. Theodosia Robertson (New York: W. W. Norton, 2004), 147.

69 "The first seed of my story 'Birds'...": ibid., 146.

69 crimson, verdigris, silver: Bruno Schulz, *The Street of Crocodiles and Other Stories*, trans. Celina Wieniewska (London: Penguin Classics, 2008), 21.

69 stony... profile: ibid., 22.

69 bronzegold: James Joyce, *Ulysses* (New York: Random House, 1934), 256.

69 pearls: ibid., 278.

69 "What beautiful music . . .": Lispector, *Água Viva*, 40.

69 "Have you ever noticed . . .": ibid., 167.

71 "decripid, poor and old": Frank Leslie, "Madame Saqui," *Frank Leslie's Ladies Magazine* 10 (1862), 540.

71 "The day of the Venetian Fête . . .": ibid., 540.

71 "The written word will take flight . . .": Assia Djebar, *Fantasia: An Algerian Cavalcade*, trans. Dorothy S. Blair (Portsmouth, NH: Heinemann, 1993), 3.

71 taking refuge . . . into the field: ibid., 10.

72 A scrap of paper . . . hand in the dark: ibid., 3.

72 She would compete . . . the highest: ibid., 10.

72 "The gale would have carried her . . .": Leslie, "Madame Saqui," 540.

72 Confidently . . . beloved rope: ibid., 540.

72 "Oh! the exhilaration . . .": Djebar, *Fantasia*, 10.

72 "those words had found their true home . . .": ibid., 61.

72 "The blue of heaven . . .": ibid., 3.

73 which conventional people . . . repulsive: Carrington, *The Hearing Trumpet*, 3.

73 "Personally . . .": ibid., 3.

73 England . . . woolly dogs: ibid., 3.

74 "How small a thought . . .": Ludwig Wittgenstein, *Culture and Value*, trans. Peter Winch (Chicago: University of Chicago Press, 1980), 50.

74 A star was waiting . . . distant past: Rilke, "The First Elegy," in *The Selected Poetry of Rainer Maria Rilke*, 151.

74 Wittgenstein took some apples . . . parts of his sentences": Wittgenstein, *Culture and Value*, 31.

75 He wondered if there was something feminine about this way of thinking: ibid., 31.

79   someone who falls . . . Place de l'Opéra: Kafka, *Diaries*, 33.

79   "visceral time": Claude Lévi-Strauss, *The Raw and the Cooked*, trans. John and Doreen Weightman (Chicago: University of Chicago Press, 1983), 16.

79   "Re-writing is writing . . .": Bhanu Kapil, deleted blog post, 2016, *The Vortex of Formidable Sparkles*, thesparklyblogof bhanukapil.blogspot.com/. Used with permission.

79   She put her hand . . . cardiac output: Bhanu Kapil, *Humanimal: A Project for Future Children* (Berkeley, CA: Kelsey Street, 2009), 12.

80   never so intimidated . . . block of ice: Claude Lévi-Strauss, *Tristes Tropiques*, trans. John and Doreen Weightman (New York: Penguin, 1992), 20.

81   to die standing up . . . glass cage: Alejandra Pizarnik, "A Selection from *Diaries*," trans. Cecilia Rossi, *Music & Literature* 6 (2015), 27.

81   "The voices burn . . .": ibid., 27.

81   "Pas compris . . .": ibid., 27.

82   "From the time of my youth . . .": Jean-Jacques Rousseau, quoted in Roland Barthes, *The Neutral*, trans. Rosalind E. Krauss and Denis Hollier (New York: Columbia University Press, 2005), 148.

82   "I was fully resolved . . .": ibid., 148.

82   "The moment having come . . .": ibid., 148.

83   "I forsook the world and its pomp . . .": ibid., 148.

83   "lets himself be tossed . . .": Barthes, *The Neutral*, 182.

84   He was walking down the road from Ménilmontant . . .: ibid., 5–6.

84   "A delicious moment . . .": ibid., 6.

84   the lofty sky . . . slowly across it: ibid., 5. Barthes is quoting

Leo Tolstoy; his translators have used *War and Peace*, trans. Louise Maude and Aylmer Maude (New York: Norton, 1966), 301–302.

85 **studium and punctum:** Roland Barthes, *Camera Lucida: Reflections on Photography*, trans. Richard Howard (New York: Farrar, Straus and Giroux, 1981), 26–27.

85 **"that accident . . .":** ibid., 27.

86 **"To be a copyist . . .":** Sarah Lehrer-Graiwer, "Concording Lozano's Private Notebooks," *Animal Shelter* 4 (2015), 27.

87 **"dedicated his scruples . . .":** Jorge Luis Borges, "Pierre Menard, Author of the *Quixote*," in *Labyrinths*, trans. James E. Irby (New York: New Directions, 1964), 44.

89 **"dedicó sus escrúpulos . . .":** Jorge Luis Borges, "Pierre Menard, autor del *Quijote*," in *Ficciones* (Buenos Aires: Emecé Editores, 1956), 55.

89 **à copier de la musique à tant la page:** Jean-Jacques Rousseau, quoted in Roland Barthes, *Le Neutre* (Paris: Éditions du Seuil, 2002), 191.

89 **transcribed texts . . . like a transparent sheet:** Enrique Vila-Matas, *Bartleby & Co.*, trans. Jonathan Dunne (New York: New Directions, 2004), 4.

89 **"como una lámina transparente":** Enrique Vila-Matas, *Bartleby y compañía* (Barcelona: Seix Barral, 2015), 14.

89 **"come una lastra trasparente":** Roberto Calasso, *I quarantanove gradini* (Milan, Italy: Adelphi edizioni, 1991), 95.

90 **"écrire . . .":** Marguerite Duras, *Écrire* (Paris: Gallimard, 1993), 34.

90 **"escribir . . .":** Vila-Matas, *Bartleby y compañía*, 26.

90 **a sinuous garland of plagiarism:** Calasso, *La Folie Baudelaire*, 7.

90 **"una sinuosa ghirlanda di plagi":** Roberto Calasso, *La folie Baudelaire* (Siena, Italy: Monte dei Paschi di Siena, 2011), 20.

90 lively eyes . . . halves of birds: Calasso, *La Folie Baudelaire*, 133.

90 metà di uccelli: Calasso, *La folie Baudelaire*, 165.

90 moitiés d'oiseaux: Charles Baudelaire, "Lettre à Charles Asselineau," in *Lettres: 1841–1866* (Mercure de France, 1907), 88.

90 bizarre, monstrous: Calasso, *La Folie Baudelaire*, 133.

90 bizzarri, mostruosi: Calasso, *La folie Baudelaire*, 166.

90 bizarres, monstrueux: Baudelaire, "Lettre à Charles Asselineau," 88.

90 *"The girl such and such . . ."*: Calasso, *La Folie Baudelaire*, 133. Italics in the original.

90 pleasing: ibid., 133.

90 molto brunito: Calasso, *La folie Baudelaire*, 166.

90 d'une couleur orientale: Baudelaire, "Lettre à Charles Asselineau," 89.

91 "This is Charing Cross Station . . .": Tayeb Salih, *Season of Migration to the North*, trans. Denys Johnson-Davies (New York: New York Review of Books, 2009), 14.

91 "very little" . . . "so much": Ford Madox Hueffer, "Antwerp" (London: Poetry Bookshop, 1915), 7.

91 "All of a sudden . . .": Salih, *Season of Migration to the North*, 14.

91 إنما و هما من الأوهام: Tayeb Salih, *Mawsim al-hijrah ila al-shamal* (Beirut, Lebanon: Dongola, 2019), 21.

91 an afreet . . . his eyes shooting out flames: Salih, *Season of Migration to the North*, 14.

92 dreamy and listless: ibid., 13.

92 حالمتين ناعستين: Salih, *Mawsim al-hijrah ila al-shamal*, 20.

92 It is to hush: Duras, *Écrire*, 34. My translation.

92 Es aullar sin ruido: Vila-Matas, *Bartleby y compañía*, 26.

93 "How, indeed . . .": Abdelfattah Kilito, *The Author and His*

Doubles: Essays on Classical Arabic Culture, trans. Michael Cooperson (Syracuse, NY: Syracuse University Press, 2001), 100.

93   "The serpent...": Al-Jahiz, *Kitab al-hayawan*, trans. Michael Cooperson, quoted in Kilito, *The Author and His Doubles*, 91.

94   "Can one...": Roland Barthes, *Roland Barthes by Roland Barthes*, trans. Richard Howard (New York: Hill and Wang, 1977), 99.

94   his way of strolling through the world... a phrase in his head: ibid., 91.

94   reading his classics... dining car: ibid., 91.

94   the way he actually saw him... reading a book!: ibid., 91–92.

95   "When someone says a word...": Mieko Kanai, reported conversation with Mina Kitahara in personal email, January 18, 2018. Used with permission.

95   "the essential sting": Roland Barthes, *The Preparation of the Novel*, trans. Kate Briggs, ed. Nathalie Léger (New York: Columbia University Press, 2011), 75.

95   "I often pursue...": Hervé Guibert, *Crazy for Vincent*, trans. Christine Pichini (Los Angeles: Semiotext(e), 2017), 62.

95   "a leather belt...": Roland Barthes, *The Fashion System*, trans. Richard Howard, quoted in Mieko Kanai, *Indian Summer*, trans. Tomoko Aoyama and Barbara Hartley (Ithaca, NY: Cornell University Press, 2012), 112.

95   "a cotton dress...": ibid., 112.

95   "gauze, organza...": ibid., 112.

96   everything visible... rounded cushion: Mieko Kanai describes a photograph from Roland Barthes's *Camera Lucida* in *Indian Summer*, 112.

96   soft and transparent... woven fabric: Kanai, *Indian Summer*, 113.

96 "I simply want to say . . .": ibid., 113.

97 "So she was considering in her own mind . . .": Lewis Carroll, *Alice's Adventures in Wonderland*, ed. Richard Kelly (Peterborough, ON: Broadview, 2011), 63.

97 "The whole place around her . . .": ibid., 158.

98 When she first read Barthes's *Camera Lucida* . . . : Kanai, *Indian Summer*, 113–14.

98 "I told Dean . . .": Jack Kerouac, *On the Road* (London: Penguin Classics, 2002), 208.

98 "Another fantasy I had . . .": Karl Ove Knausgaard, *My Struggle: Book One*, trans. Don Bartlett (New York: Farrar, Straus and Giroux, 2012), 274.

99 "I remember when I was a kid . . .": Sofia Samatar, *Tender: Stories* (Small Beer, 2017), 176.

99 "I was leveling the whole country . . .": ibid., 176.

100 "I always stood in fear . . .": Jorge Luis Borges, *Borges at 80: Conversations*, ed. Willis Barnstone (Bloomington: Indiana University Press, 1982), 153.

102 "a second-rate literary form": Sara Steinert Borella, *The Travel Narratives of Ella Maillart: (En)Gendering the Quest* (New York: Peter Lang, 2006), 2.

102 "a problem for academic studies" . . . "contingent . . .": ibid., 5.

103 "Everything I achieve . . .": Robert Walser, *Microscripts*, trans. Susan Bernofsky (New York: New Directions, 2012), 51.

103 vaulted . . . train": ibid., 91.

103 rushed headlong . . . district: ibid., 92–93.

103 what Édouard Glissant might have called its *opacity*: Édouard Glissant, "For Opacity," in *Poetics of Relation*, trans. Betsy Wing (Ann Arbor: University of Michigan Press, 1997), 189–94.

105 "If words are to be uttered . . .": Cha, *Dictee*, 132.

106 Samuel R. Delany, who said . . . who were not black: Samuel R. Delany, "Racism and Science Fiction," in *Dark Matter: A Century of Speculative Fiction from the African Diaspora*, ed. Sheree R. Thomas (New York: Warner Books, 2000), 396.

106 he was happy to speak with her: ibid., 395.

106 "You want to join . . .": Ama Ata Aidoo, *Our Sister Killjoy* (New York: Longman, 1977), 10.

106 two extremely handsome Nigerian men: ibid., 10.

106 "Things are working out . . .": ibid., 3–4.

106 The flight was arranged . . . sunshine: ibid., 10.

108 a political humanist and an intellectual anti-humanist: Stuart Hall, quoted in Lawrence Grossberg, "Affect's Future: Rediscovering the Virtual in the Actual," in *The Affect Theory Reader*, ed. Melissa Gregg and Gregory J. Seigworth (Durham, NC: Duke University Press, 2010), 331.

108 "that neutral power . . .": Maurice Blanchot, *The Gaze of Orpheus and Other Literary Essays*, trans. Lydia Davis (Barrytown, NY: Station Hill, 1981), 71.

108 "no longer capable . . .": ibid., 72.

109 "Experiments have proved . . .": Benjamin, *Illuminations*, 137.

109 When she was twenty-three . . . Some other person is writing this: Kanai, *The Word Book*, 42.

112 "Slept, awoke, slept . . .": Kafka, *Diaries*, 14.

112 When I think about it . . . more than I can conceive: ibid., 14–16, 18, 21–22.

112 "When I look back like this . . .": ibid., 29.

114 "The stones preserve . . .": Rainer Maria Rilke, *Auguste Rodin*, trans. Jessie Lemont and Hans Trausil (New York: Sunwise Turn, 1919), 77.

115 one of those ribbands of stone . . . overflows: ibid., 70.

116 "I know that I have mentioned this already . . .": Clarice

Lispector, *The Foreign Legion*, trans. Giovanni Pontiero (New York: New Directions, 1992), 132.

117 **"decanted"**: Susan Rubin Suleiman, "Writing Past the Wall, or the Passion According to H. C.," in Hélène Cixous, *"Coming to Writing" and Other Essays*, ed. Deborah Jenson (Cambridge, MA: Harvard University Press, 1991), viii.

117 **she wanted to be a painter**: Hélène Cixous, "The Last Painting or the Portrait of God," in *"Coming to Writing" and Other Essays*, 104–31.

117 **to paint the cathedral twenty-six times . . . in all its lights**: ibid., 110.

117 **"My sleep was filled with nightmares . . ."**: Claude Monet, quoted in Cixous, "The Last Painting or the Portrait of God," 110.

117 **"I continue to draw . . ."**: Katsushika Hokusai, quoted in Cixous, "The Last Painting or the Portrait of God," 124.

117 **She quoted Jean Genet . . . his last paintings**: Cixous, "The Last Painting or the Portrait of God," 115.

117 **"Art is not purity . . ."**: Clarice Lispector, *Loud Object*, trans. Benjamin Moser, quoted in Benjamin Moser, *Why This World: A Biography of Clarice Lispector* (New York: Oxford University Press, 2009), 317.

117 **the Isaac Watts hymn about purifying the heart**: Isaac Watts, "Almighty Maker, God!," in *The Church Hymn Book for the Worship of God*, ed. Edwin F. Hatfield (New York: Ivison, Blakeman, Taylor, 1873), 88.

118 **"It is only at the end . . ."**: Cixous, "The Last Painting or the Portrait of God," 115.

119 **"What do copyists . . ."**: Kilito, *The Author and His Doubles*, 87.

119 **"I lay on my back . . ."**: ibid., 87.

120 **"Is Cézanne's concern . . ."**: Maurice Blanchot, *The Space of*

Literature, trans. Ann Smock (Lincoln: University of Nebraska Press, 1982), 235.

120 **with a certainty** . . . **cease to hurt:** Hugo von Hofmannsthal, *The Lord Chandos Letter*, trans. Ann Smock, quoted in Blanchot, *The Space of Literature*, 183.

120 **"This much no one can doubt . . .":** ibid., 235.

IV: NIGHT

123 **"My work was only created . . .":** Stéphane Mallarmé, letter to Eugène Lefébure, quoted in Barthes, *The Preparation of the Novel*, 47. Barthes's translator notes that Barthes has miscopied the text slightly, so that "its liberated shadows" becomes "the timbres it emitted." See Barthes, *The Preparation of the Novel*, 418.

123 **"Destruction was my Beatrice":** Mallarmé, quoted in Barthes, *The Preparation of the Novel*, 47.

124 **"I need solitude . . .":** Franz Kafka, *Letters to Felice*, trans. James Stern and Elisabeth Duckworth (New York: Schocken Classics, 2016), 279.

124 **Two boys were sitting . . . sword on high:** Franz Kafka, "The Hunter Gracchus," trans. Willa and Edwin Muir, in *Franz Kafka: The Complete Stories*, 226.

124 **A girl filled her bucket . . . gazing at the lake:** ibid., 226.

124 **"telling the accidental . . .":** Stanley Cavell, *Little Did I Know: Excerpts from Memory* (Stanford: Stanford University Press, 2010), 5.

124 **Through the vacant window . . . dozing:** Kafka, "The Hunter Gracchus," 226.

124 **The bark was silently . . . over the water:** ibid., 226.

125 **"Anyone who cannot cope with life . . .":** Franz Kafka, trans. Hannah Arendt, quoted in Arendt, "Walter Benjamin: 1892–1940," 19.

125 A man in a blue blouse . . . the real survivor: Kafka, "The Hunter Gracchus," 226.

126 "If I have to die . . .": Kanai, *The Word Book*, 137.

127 "Like a little work of art . . .": Friedrich Schlegel, quoted in Jacques Derrida, *Points . . . Interviews, 1974–1994*, trans. Peggy Kamuf (Stanford, CA: Stanford University Press, 1995), 302.

127 his right hand . . . forehead: Friedrich Schlegel, *Friedrich Schlegel's* Lucinde *and the Fragments*, trans. Peter Firchow (Minneapolis: University of Minnesota Press, 1971), 54.

127 a narrow, dark corridor . . . a sort of salon: Benjamin, *The Arcades Project*, 925.

127 "On the pale-colored wallpaper . . .": ibid., 925.

127 "Occasionally . . .": Rilke, *The Notebooks of Malte Laurids Brigge*, 45.

129 "Ah," he wrote, "if that were enough . . .": ibid., 45.

129 For weeks now . . . in the night: ibid., 183.

130 He wakened in himself . . . crêpe de Chine: Roland Barthes, *Camera Lucida*, 65.

130 "As I removed the second period . . .": Kapil, *Schizophrene*, 72.

130 "*forcibly excluded*": Edward W. Said, *Culture and Imperialism* (New York: Vintage Books, 1994), 67. Emphasis added.

131 "To puncture to scratch . . .": Cha, *Dictee*, 65.

133 "Intensity" . . . "Cold or hot . . .": Octavia E. Butler, "Notes on Writing, ca. 1970–1995" (San Marino, CA: The Huntington Library, Art Collections, and Botanical Gardens, 2016). Copyright: Estate of Octavia E. Butler.

133 "The world is too small . . .": Anaïs Nin, *House of Incest* (Athens, OH: Swallow, 1989), 44.

133 In the train once . . . to weep: Anaïs Nin, "from *Winter of Artifice*," in *Anaïs Nin Reader*, ed. Philip K. Jason (Chicago: Swallow Press, 1973), 45.

133 "I'd like to write a story . . .": Lispector, "Six Letters from Clarice Lispector," 27.

134 If you don't stop crying . . . hear her sobs: Nin, "from *Winter of Artifice*," 45–46.

134 "You never saw the stars . . .": Nin, *House of Incest*, 44.

134 She sobbed all the way to Berlin: Nin, "from *Winter of Artifice*," 46.

136 "If there is one idea . . .": Kanai, *The Word Book*, 9.

137 "Until today . . .": Lispector, *The Foreign Legion*, 127.

137 if she could finish . . . not worry about how many: Lispector, *The Passion According to G. H.*, 155.

137 "If only I could write . . .": Lispector, *The Foreign Legion*, 211.

137 the blue dress . . . a little thinner: Lispector, *The Passion According to G. H.*, 155.

138 "I have only existed . . .": Vila-Matas, *Bartleby & Co.*, 176–77.

140 "But my sole ambition . . .": Djebar, *Fantasia*, 63.

141 "Every great spirit . . .": Victor Hugo, quoted in Benjamin, *The Arcades Project*, 775.

141 the hounds and the foxes . . . nature shuddering: ibid., 775–76.

141 "Without understanding the reason . . .": Anna Kavan, *Sleep Has His House* (London: Peter Owen, 2002), 55.

141 keep the day world . . . waited for the night: ibid., 55.

141 She grew taller and thinner . . . blank window: ibid., 23.

141 she *had to* establish reality in another place: ibid., 75. Emphasis added.

141 Words took fright . . . the lamp was afraid: Victor Hugo, quoted in Benjamin, *The Arcades Project*, 776.

141 "Get up! . . .": ibid., 775.

141 she struck out . . . night-plasma: Kavan, *Sleep Has His House*, 8.

142 no sound . . . sea or land: ibid., 9.

142 going home to her night world: ibid., 55.

143 "O night without objects": Rilke, *The Notebooks of Malte Laurids Brigge*, 69.

143 In the evenings . . . timorous and beautiful: ibid., 130–31.

144 "All night long . . .": Pizarnik, *Extracting the Stone of Madness*, 47.

145 "The burning electric light . . .": Kafka, *Diaries*, 39.

145 hurriedly . . . the person he was: ibid., 39.

145 *I* is only a word . . . the telephone: Lispector, *The Foreign Legion*, 51.

145 "*I am* may have been . . .": Leonora Carrington, "What is a Woman?" in *Surrealist Women: An International Anthology*, ed. Penelope Rosemont (Austin: University of Texas Press, 1998), 373.

145 "If I am my thoughts . . .": ibid., 373.

145 a million tiny . . . in order to miss nothing: Rilke, *The Notebooks of Malte Laurids Brigge*, 173.

147 "I just need to be able to look . . .": Lispector, *The Passion According to G. H.*, 19.

147 She felt that there was something . . . see too much: Lispector, "Six Letters from Clarice Lispector," 27.

147 such perfume! It was Sunday morning: Lispector, *The Foreign Legion*, 185.

147 "And I also have no name . . .": Lispector, *The Passion According to G. H.*, 169.

149 "My final word . . .": Pizarnik, *Extracting the Stone of Madness*, 69.

150 he spoke only to those . . . facing the dawn: Schlegel, *Friedrich Schlegel's* Lucinde *and the Fragments*, 254.

150 "Every doctrine . . .": ibid., 256.

151 "So long as writing . . .": Mieko Kanai, "Rabbits," trans. Olivia Martin, *Olivia's Translations*, 2014, oliviastranslations

.blogspot.com/2014/07/rabbits-by-kanai-mieko.html. Used with permission.

151 It was still early morning . . . depths of her lungs: Kanai, *The Word Book*, 113.

153 "Does each book . . .": Sergio Pitol, *The Art of Flight*, trans. George Henson (Dallas: Deep Vellum, 2015), 220.

153 "At the onset . . .": Rainer Maria Rilke, *Letters to a Young Painter*, trans. Damion Searls (New York: David Zwirner, 2017), 47.

153 It was night . . . he was freezing: Rilke, *The Notebooks of Malte Laurids Brigge*, 182.

153 "you must seek . . .": Rilke, *Letters to a Young Painter*, 47.

153 "She says to herself . . .": Cha, *Dictee*, 141.

154 spontaneous things that were happening everywhere: Rilke, *The Notebooks of Malte Laurids Brigge*, 173.

154 as agreeably tired . . . Ulsgaard: ibid., 23.

154 in the cool freshness . . . spiritual transparency: ibid., 173.

SOFIA SAMATAR is a writer of fiction and nonfiction, including the memoir *The White Mosque*, a PEN/Jean Stein Award finalist. Her works range from the World Fantasy Award–winning novel *A Stranger in Olondria* to *Tone*, a study of literary tone with Kate Zambreno. Samatar lives in Virginia and teaches African literature, Arabic literature, and speculative fiction at James Madison University.